Loosen THE Grip

Loosen THE Grip

STRATEGIES FOR RAISING
INDEPENDENT AND **CONFIDENT**
CRITICAL THINKERS

LISA K. ANDERSON

 *Advantage* | Books

Published by Advantage, Charleston, South Carolina.
Member of Advantage Media.

ADVANTAGE is a registered trademark, and the Advantage colophon is a trademark of Advantage Media Group, Inc.

Printed in the United States of America.

10 9 8 7 6 5 4 3 2 1

ISBN: 978-1-64225-697-0 (Paperback)
ISBN: 978-1-64225-696-3 (eBook)

Library of Congress Control Number: 2023908996

Cover design by Analisa Smith.
Layout design by Lance Buckley.

This publication is designed to provide accurate and authoritative information in regard to the subject matter covered. It is sold with the understanding that the publisher is not engaged in rendering legal, accounting, or other professional services. If legal advice or other expert assistance is required, the services of a competent professional person should be sought.

To protect the privacy of certain individuals, names and identifying details in many stories and case studies have been changed.

Advantage Media helps busy entrepreneurs, CEOs, and leaders write and publish a book to grow their business and become the authority in their field. Advantage authors comprise an exclusive community of industry professionals, idea-makers, and thought leaders. Do you have a book idea or manuscript for consideration? We would love to hear from you at **AdvantageMedia.com**.

For Steve and Amethyst, love you both.

Contents

♥

Introduction

♥

*When little people are overwhelmed by big emotions, it's
our job to share our calm, not to join their chaos.*

—L. R. KNOST

If you picked up this book to "fix" your child, put it down and walk
away. This book is not for you.

If you picked up this book because you want to be a better parent
and you are ready to own what really needs to be fixed (it's not your
child), welcome to *Loosen the Grip: Strategies for Raising Independent
and Confident Critical Thinkers.*

I'm Lisa K. Anderson, a parent, grandparent, and Licensed Professional Counselor (LPC) with a bachelor's degree in social work, a
master's degree in community counseling, and over twenty-five years
of experience counseling children and families—and still, I totally
screw up as a parent sometimes. When my daughter was three, when
she was six, and when she was eighteen—I made some *major* parenting
mistakes, and I've made a bunch of little ones in between. So I'm not
here to judge; I'm here to help you get to where you need to be: the
best parent for *your* child.

Parenting is hard. It's hard mentally, physically, and emotionally.
We love our children deeply and want only the best for them, and

still, despite our best intentions, we can lose sight of their needs and begin parenting in a way that fills our needs.

By the time my daughter was six, I had been working in earnest on my parenting skills for three years. I had been in therapy for my own childhood traumas and had been studying parenting best practices. I was putting in the work to parent my daughter in a way that was meeting her needs, or so I thought. When she was in first grade, the advisors at her school expressed concern that she had ADHD. I took her to a psychologist who, after months of testing, diagnosed her with "BRAT syndrome." It took me a minute to realize what he meant. He was saying that my daughter was a brat. My defenses immediately went up. "What do you mean my daughter is a brat?" I demanded.

"I've never seen you say no to your child in the six months you've both been coming here."

"Well, there's been no reason to say no to her."

"Oh, there've been many reasons she should have been told no," he replied.

Then he started listing them all off, and I was like, "Oh, my daughter is a brat."

I went home and asked my husband, "Do you think that I've made our daughter into a brat?"

"Yes," was his immediate reply.

I was taken aback. "What do you mean?"

"Any time I try to discipline her or tell her no, you immediately undermine me or jump in and tell me that that's not how we're going to do it. So, yes. You have made her into a brat."

It wasn't my daughter's needs that I was filling at all. It was my own needs based on my childhood experiences and expectations and what felt right for me. That's a tough pill to swallow for any parent, and I struggled with it. But once I had the courage to own it, I realized

I also had the power to be the solution; I could create a better outcome for me and my child, and you can too.

Through my practice working with families, I have seen an alarming pattern of hypervigilant parenting that results in children—even as old as seventeen and eighteen—who are in no way prepared to be independent adults. What we seem to have forgotten is that *our number one job as parents is to raise our children to be independent and self-sufficient adults*. Today, too many children lack critical-thinking and problem-solving skills, the ability to regulate their emotions, and the self-confidence to find their way in the world.

I've worked with twelve-year-olds who are throwing up in my office because they received a B-plus instead of an A on their assignment and their parents have let them know how disappointed they are, seven-year-olds who are afraid to play freely on the playground because their parents have ingrained them with all the ways they could get hurt if they aren't extremely careful, and fifteen-year-olds who don't know how to make themselves a simple meal or do their own laundry. These children have not developed the ability to make their own decisions, and in many cases, they don't know what they truly want for themselves because their parents have dictated what they want, and they don't even realize that they can have their own thoughts, ideas, and dreams.

So what pushes a parent to raise their children with hypervigilance? Parenting in a way that, often unconsciously, is fulfilling their needs rather than their children's needs. Here are the three most common needs-based parenting practices that I have observed:

- Dependency-based needs: Parents who insist on doing everything for their child to fulfill the parent's need to be needed, to keep their child dependent on them.

- Fear-based needs: Parents who are focused on keeping their child from any circumstance that may cause them any level of perceived harm, to fulfill their own fear of feeling unsafe.

- Reward-based needs: Parents who focus on controlling their child and their environment so that they behave, achieve, and appear to the level that fulfills the parent's need for perfection and image.

The good news is that all these unhealthy parenting practices can be replaced with healthy ones. It takes hard work and commitment to the long game, but I promise it's worth it.

If you're ready to roll up your sleeves, face some hard truths, and commit to making changes that will help you become the best parent for *your* child, keep reading. In these pages you will find information to help you better understand your child's development, case studies and exercises that will help you find your way, and resources to support you in the most difficult of parenting moments. Remember, there is no one "right way" to parent, and there is no perfect parent. There is only you meeting your child's needs in the best way possible. Now, let's get started.

CHAPTER 1

Is It Possible to Parent Too Much?

Loving a child doesn't mean giving in to all his whims; to love him is to bring out the best in him, to teach him to love what is difficult.

—NADIA BOULANGER

Most of us parent in some variation of the way we were parented. When we add to that our own childhood traumas, generational parenting philosophies, and the constant judgments and unrealistic expectations on social media, determining how best to parent our children can be confusing and overwhelming. We are bombarded with all the things we "should" fear as parents— abductions and sexual assaults around every corner—and all the things "good" parents "should" do for their children. Never let your child do without … anything, never let your child fail or have hurt feelings, and keep your child busy every minute of every day. I'm exaggerating a bit, but honestly, it's been my experience as an LPC that I'm not that far off. What I've described is a parenting trap that's easy to fall into. It's called *hypervigilant parenting*, and yes, it's possible to parent too much.

But before we delve into the details of hypervigilant parenting, I want to first talk about parenting on a spectrum.

RANGE OF BALANCE

Detached ├———————————————┤ Dependency-Based Needs

Abusive ├———————————————┤ Fear-Based Needs

Neglectful ├———————————————┤ Reward-Based Needs

The goal is to find the balance far from the two dysfunctional extremes. Let's first look at what each of these extremes mean.

- Detached: Parents with limited emotional attachment to their child, who tend to their child in a basic, almost mechanical way.

- Abusive: Parents who physically, emotionally, and/or sexually abuse their children.

- Neglectful: Parents who do not provide for their child's basic needs of food, shelter, clothing, safety, and love.

On the other end of the spectrum:

- Dependency-based needs: Parents who care for their children in a way that fulfills the parent's need to be needed, to keep their child dependent on them.

- Fear-based needs: Parents who care for their children in a way that fulfills the parent's need to protect their child from all perceived harm. Decisions are based on parents' own fears.

- Reward-based needs: Parents who care for their children in a way that fulfills their own need to achieve and portray a certain image.

Parents who parent based on their dependency-based, fear-based, or reward-based needs tend to do so with hypervigilance. For parents trying to fill their dependency-based needs, they insist on doing everything for their child so they will always be dependent on their help.

Fear-based needs are filled by keeping a child from any circumstance that may cause them any level of harm, and reward-based needs are filled by controlling a child and their environment so that they behave, achieve, and appear to the level of perfection the parent expects.

Balance is not a single point on the spectrum; it is a range, because parenting requires nuances that fit not only the situation but the individual child and the age and abilities of the child. Let me give you a couple of examples.

> Balance is not a single point on the spectrum.

Your three-year-old and five-year-old are playing when they start to fight over a toy. Your instinct is to jump in and resolve before the fight gets any worse (fear-based needs). But you don't. You take a step back (detach a little bit) and provide them the opportunity to try to work it out on their own. Surprise! They're successful! They may not have resolved it the way you would have wanted them to, but it works for them. You found the balance that provided your children increased confidence and independence while remaining safe.

Sometimes parenting requires a bit of overinvolvement. When my daughter was nineteen, her first love broke her heart. The night her boyfriend broke up with her, I found her crying in a fetal position under the dining room table. She was already a bit fragile because she had been struggling with a bit of anxiety through her first year of college and being away from all her friends. What did I do as her mom? I wiped her tears, put her in my bed, and held her until she fell asleep, something that I hadn't done since she was a small child. But on that night, it was exactly what she needed. And I hovered a bit for the next few days to make sure she was OK. I found the balance that provided my daughter the level of love and support that she needed in that moment.

You're not always going to get it right; no parent does. I know I have veered too far to either side of the spectrum at times. What sometimes seems like the right balance in the moment turns out to be too extreme in hindsight. It will happen. Gain insight from those experiences and draw on them the next time you're trying to determine the best approach to a parenting challenge.

> ## TAKE A MOMENT
>
> Make a list of three parenting "mistakes" you've made in the past year. They can be major or minor mistakes. They can all be with the same child or three mistakes with three different children. That's it; just list them and put them aside for later.

Loosening the Grip: Increasing Independence

Meet "Tom," a thirteen-year-old boy whose mom was afraid to let him go anywhere alone. Tom and his siblings had limited freedom and independence; Mom went with them virtually everywhere. At one point, Tom had a soccer practice that conflicted with his mom's schedule. Tom and his friend suggested they ride their bikes there after school. It was less than two miles away and Tom knew the way.

His mom pushed back. Her rationale for saying no came down to two things:

1. Fear-based needs: Her son could be abducted en route. Mom was parenting based on her own fears.

2. Rewards-based needs: "I'd look like a horrible mother if he rides his bike to practice. Parents drive their children everywhere." Mom was parenting based on her need to project the proper image.

8

Let's break down Mom's rationale in this scenario.

FEAR-BASED NEEDS

In today's world, we are bombarded with stories of child abduction. These are very real happenings in the world that we must take seriously, but we must also base those fears in reality.

Reality:

- On average, fewer than 350 people under the age of twenty-one have been abducted by strangers in the United States per year since 2010, the FBI says. [1]

- From 2010 through 2017, the most recent data available, the number has ranged from a low of 303 in 2016 to a high of 384 in 2011 with no clear directional trend. [2]

- Family kidnappings make up half of all reported abductions in the United States, and 27 percent are abductions by acquaintances. [3]

That means only 23 percent of child abductions are committed by strangers. Again, I am not minimizing the danger of child abductions—they are real—but the chances of your child being snatched off the street by a stranger are very low, and yet the fear of stranger abduction is driving parents to severely limit their children's freedom at significant expense to their children's well-being.

These types of driving fears lead parents to overvalue risk and undervalue rewards. The consequence? Parents who are more focused

1   Reuters, "Kidnapped Children Make Headlines, but Abduction Is Rare in U.S.," January 11, 2019, https://www.reuters.com/article/us-wisconsin-missinggirl-data/kidnapped-children-make-headlines-but-abduction-is-rare-in-u-s-idUSKCN1P52BJ.

2   Ibid.

3   Child Crime Prevention and Safety Center, "Missing and Abducted Children," accessed April 10, 2023, https://childsafety.losangelescriminallawyer.pro/missing-and-abducted-children.html.

on their own fears about what might happen to their children more than they are on what their children might gain from an experience. Tom and his mom are a perfect example, and they are not alone.

REWARD-BASED NEEDS

Now let's look at the second rationale that Tom's mom gave for not letting him ride his bike to the practice: image. Worrying about what others may think of us is not new, but in the age of social media and cyberbullying, this concern is in hyperdrive. Like the consequences of parenting based on unrealistic fears, parenting based on the projection of a certain image that is rooted in unrealistic expectations is limiting our children's confidence and independence. Demanding that children live up to unattainable expectations leads to incredible stress and a sense of constant failure, of never being enough.

Teen girls using social media five or more hours per day displayed a 50 percent increase in depressive symptoms compared to girls using social media one to three hours per day. Teen boys displayed a 35 percent increase.[4]

SETTING UP FOR SUCCESS

The fears and unrealistic expectations of Tom's mom aren't going to be resolved overnight, but in this instance, there were a few simple steps that could provide guidance for Tom and serve to assuage some of his mother's concerns.

---

4   Katie Hurley, "Social Media and Depression: Research Links the Problems, Especially in Teens," PSYCOM, June 8, 2022, https://www.psycom.net/depression/depression-in-teens/social-media-and-teenage-depression.

3. Tom felt confident that he could ride his bike from his school to the soccer field.

4. Mom emailed the soccer coach in advance and let them know that Tom would be riding his bike to practice and that she would pick him up.

5. Tom agreed to "check in" with his mom via text at different intervals so that she knew he was fine.

Tom made it to his practice, and his mom arrived to pick him up just as practice was finishing. When I talked to him about how it went, he was so proud of himself for not only getting there but having the courage to go alone when his friend canceled at the last minute. He debated on what to do and decided to text his mom that he was going alone and then texted her when he arrived at the field. Now he was ready to talk to his mom about riding his bike to practice on a regular basis. Through this experience, Tom gained self-confidence, learned life skills, and improved his relationship with his mom.

How Hypervigilant Parenting Shows Up

There are a variety of ways in which our own needs can manifest in unhealthy parenting behaviors. We've looked at one of those ways in the case of Tom's mother, who was overvaluing risk (Tom would be abducted if she didn't drive him everywhere) and undervaluing rewards (Tom at thirteen needed to exercise some independence and boost his self-confidence).

Being driven by fear often means that parents are not allowing children to participate in certain age-appropriate activities that are necessary for children to gain experience and develop independence and self-efficacy to grow up to be self-sufficient adults.

Here are some examples of age-appropriate activities:

- Pre-K: Be dropped off at a friend's house to play.

- Age 4 and up: Go to day camp (sleepover camp is appropriate for most kids starting around age 8).

- Age 6 and up: Walk a few blocks alone in their neighborhood.

- Age 7 and up: Go ahead of you at the grocery store to find an item in the next aisle.

- Ages 11 to 14: Be dropped off at an appropriate location with friends like the library, a movie, or the mall.

When you read over that list, how did you feel? Does the idea of letting your seven-year-old go ahead of you to the next aisle in the grocery store make you start to hyperventilate? What about dropping your twelve-year-old off at the movies with friends? Sit with those feelings and try to figure out why they make you feel the way you do. Where are your fears coming from, and are they based in reality?

Now let's talk about a few other signs of hypervigilant parenting: expecting perfection, overscheduling, inappropriate age expectations, and lack of consequences.

EXPECTING PERFECTION

The desire to want the best *for* their children often means parents demand the best *from* their children. That *best* is often perfection—something no one can attain. I once had a fourteen-year-old throwing up in my office because he was getting a B in one of his classes and he knew that his parents would ground him because they would not accept anything less than an A. "Seth" knew that his parents would pull him from every activity that he liked, including playing sports and hanging out with his friends, because of that one B. He said, "I'm going to have to sit and do nothing but homework all summer long. What's the point of living?" Seth had been referred to me because he had been suicidal, and yet his parents were unable to acknowledge their role in this downward spiral and were instead looking for ways to "fix" their son.

As adults, we may consider his comment about "the point of living" if he had to stay in and do homework all summer a bit melodramatic, but I assure you it was a very real mindset for Seth.

Parents who expect perfection from their children often expect the same for themselves, even though we logically know

> # Parents who expect perfection from their children often expect the same for themselves.

that attaining perfection in everything we do is *not* possible. We know it, yet we continue to strive for it. Parents who were raised with the expectation of being perfect or who have bought into social media's push to be perfect—or at least appear to be perfect—will be challenged to not put that same unrealistic expectation on their children.

OVERSCHEDULING

Not wanting their children to miss out on opportunities, parents often pack their children's schedule with activities and lessons, which means children are rushing from one organized event to the next with little or no free time for themselves or to be with friends. Eventually these children start to not want to do these activities, and when their requests to stop are ignored, they become what parents see as oppositional and defiant, or they start becoming physically ill or anxious. Overscheduled teenagers often end up sleep deprived because they are forced to "sneak in" free time or time talking with their friends late into the night but still need to get up early the next morning to start the cycle all over again.

Loosening the Grip: Creating Free Time

Meet "Lucy," a seven-year-old girl whose mom had a busy schedule—a schedule that Lucy had to fit into, which meant getting up at five-thirty in the morning to be at before-school care at six. School started for Lucy at eight and then she attended after-school care from three to five. Mom picked Lucy up after work, and they went home and had dinner. Once dinner was over, it was back in the car to drive her older brother to practice and then run errands with her mom, then back to pick up her brother. Once back home, it was time for bed. While Lucy didn't have to go to school on the weekends, that time was still spent running errands with her mom and getting her brother to and from his games and practices.

SETTING UP FOR SUCCESS

This schedule was no one's fault; it's simply the schedule of a single parent working full time and raising two children. But by stepping back, we were able to come up with some ideas that got Lucy out of the car and provided her the opportunity for the free playtime that every kid needs:

1. Lucy's grandparents lived in a nearby neighborhood. Mom had been reluctant to ask them to watch Lucy out of concern that it would be too much for them, and in the back of her mind was this thought that needing help made her an incompetent parent. We talked through how even competent parents need help sometimes,

and that she should let her parents decide whether they were able to help or not. When asked, Lucy's grandparents were more than happy to have Lucy come to their house after school three days a week. There were kids Lucy's age in the neighborhood, and so she was able to make friends to play with while there.

2. Mom had another single-parent friend who lived nearby, and they started doing a swap. One Saturday the kids would hang out at the friend's house, and the next Saturday they would stay at Lucy's.

Mom was lucky to have her parents' assistance, something not every parent has, and these new arrangements got Lucy out of the car and playing and allowed Mom the freedom to get things done.

What Are the Appropriate Expectations for Your Child?

Below is an age-appropriate chore chart from yourmodernfamily.com that I frequently share with parents. It's important to note that inappropriate expectations works both ways: expecting too much and expecting too little. Expecting more than they are developmentally capable of creates fear and anxiety and chips away at a child's self-confidence. On the other end, a child who is not taught to be a helping member of the family is not going to know how to be a helping member of any other group they belong to. Performing age-appropriate chores builds skills and competencies that in turn build confidence.

If children are led to believe that adults are there to wait on them hand and foot, they will be in for a rude awakening when they start school and expect that their teacher will do the same.

AGE-APPROPRIATE CHORES FOR CHILDREN

Ages 2-3

- Pick up the blankets
- Put toys away
- Throw away trash
- Put the books on the bookshelf
- Help set the table
- Pick up the pillows on the floor
- Fold the washcloths
- Put dirty clothes in the hamper
- Dust the baseboards
- Get the diapers and wipes from the basket
- Carry firewood

Ages 4-5

- Make your bed
- Clean out everything under your bed
- Feed the pets
- Pick up toys
- Dry dishes and put away the ones you can reach
- Dust the furniture
- Clear and clean table after dinner
- Make easy snacks
- Wipe down doorknobs
- Weed the garden

Ages 6-7

- Sweep the kitchen floor
- Empty the dishwasher
- Sweep the upstairs hallway
- Mop the kitchen floor
- Get the trash from the bedrooms and bathrooms
- Rake leaves
- Fold clothes and match socks
- Make a simple salad
- Peel carrots and potatoes
- Organize the mudroom storage area

Ages 8-9

- Wash your own laundry
- Walk the dogs
- Bring the empty garbage cans up from the curb
- Put groceries away
- Wipe bathroom sink and vanity
- Sweep the front porch
- Sweep the back porch
- Hang, fold, and put away clean clothes
- Make scrambled eggs
- Bake cookies
- Change light bulbs

Ages 10 -11

- Clean the toilets (inside and outside)
- Sweep the garage and driveway
- Bring the mail inside
- Wash mirrors
- Clean the steps with a broom and then a damp rag (wooden steps) or with a small, handheld vacuum (carpeted steps)
- Make a simple meal
- Wipe down counters
- Clean kitchen

Ages 12+

- Clean the garage
- Clean and detail cars inside and out
- Mow the lawn
- Clean glass items
- Change overhead lights
- Iron clothes
- Watch younger siblings
- Mop the floors
- Wash windows
- Cook a complete meal
- Help with simple home repairs
- Help grocery shop
- Paint

Our role as parents is to prepare our children to grow up and live independently in the world, and that world is full of consequences—positive and negative. Without consequences children won't learn from their mistakes or understand how their actions affect not only them but the world around them. Setting consequences for poor behavior and sticking to them can be challenging. Allowing for natural consequences will be more impactful and less punitive. Here's an example.

Consequences are simply a way to teach your children the results of their actions.

Your son's chore is to do the laundry, he doesn't do it. You end up having to do the laundry that afternoon. Later, he asks you for a ride to his friend's. Because he chose not to do his chore, which meant you had to do it, you do not have time to give him a ride. It's not a punishment and not a lecture; it's simply the natural consequence of a choice he made.

> Consequences are simply a way to teach your children the results of their actions.

"Dad, can you give me a ride to the movies?"

"I'd love to, but because I had to spend time doing your chore, I won't have time to give you a ride. You'll have to find a different way to get there."

When the son argues back, the dad just needs to calmly state that he is simply needing to do the chore that his son chose not to do. Often, we get in the habit of taking things away in response to a behavior even if one isn't related to the other. Your child doesn't do their homework, so you take away their video game. Unless they are not getting their homework done *because* they spent too much time playing video games, then that consequence is unnatural and punitive. If they get a detention or poor grade at school because they didn't get their homework done, that is a natural consequence. If a pattern develops with any behavior, you need to determine the root cause.

I know that the energy it takes to not give in can be exhausting. But not setting consequences or repeatedly giving in to the ones you have set can have long-term negative costs for your child. I've had moms tell me that their son or daughter called them a bitch. When I ask what the consequence was, they will say, "They didn't mean it. They were just mad." While that may be true, they still must be held accountable for their disrespectful behavior. When they go out into the world and are disrespectful to their teacher or boss in the same way, they will face real consequences—consequences for which they are not prepared.

Reinforced by Communities

Hypervigilant parenting is often reinforced by the communities we rely on for guidance about our children. Schools are quick to label kids (gifted, delinquent, etc.) and treat them accordingly. The fear of these negative labels and the pressure of the positive labels can push parents to extremes to make sure their child either isn't given a negative label or maintains the standard of a positive label at all costs. This looks only at behavior and not at how kids think, what they feel, their capabilities, situations influencing them, or the root causes of their behavior.

School is not the only community where this may occur. Playgrounds, birthday parties, and extracurricular activities also create opportunities for children to be labeled or for parents to behave out of concern for how they may be judged. Parents may be embarrassed if their child isn't the best athlete or if they cannot afford to allow their child to give an expensive birthday gift to their friend. These are all things that a parent must be aware of, and they must "check" themselves to make sure they are parenting on what is best for their child and not on filling their own needs.

How can we do better as parents? Let's first look at our child's developing brain and how we can create a healthy environment for them to learn and grow.

REFLECTION: HOW ARE YOU PARENTING?

- Take out that list of parenting "mistakes" you made. Place each one where you think they fall on the range of balance below:

RANGE OF BALANCE

Detached |——————————| Dependency-Based Needs

Abusive |——————————| Fear-Based Needs

Neglectful |——————————| Reward-Based Needs

Now put each mistake under the appropriate category(s) below and begin to think about your role in creating that category.

- Expecting perfection
- Overscheduling
- Inappropriate age expectations
- Lack of consequences

CHAPTER 2

Why Is Hypervigilance a Problem for My Child?

The parent who is willing to bail their child out of every difficulty may be doing him or her a devastating disservice.

—DR. JAMES DOBSON

To understand the negative effects of hypervigilant parenting on a child and how to develop a positive parenting path forward, we must first have a basic understanding of the neurobiology of child development. From that framework of knowledge, you will be able to determine the best way to parent *your* child based on *your* child's needs and abilities as they grow. There is not a magical one-size-fits-all parenting method. My goal is to share a variety of parenting tips, techniques, and insights based on how a child's brain develops so that you can choose to adopt the ones that are best for your child's healthy development and fine-tune them as needed for you and your child.

The Neurobiology of Our Developing Brains

When a baby is first born, all they're really functioning with is their brain stem. The brain stem is what connects our brain to our spine, and its purpose is to regulate our automatic functions that keep us alive. The stem is how we breathe, regulate our body temperature, blink, and defend ourselves against potential harm—our automated flight, fight, or freeze responses.

Our limbic emotional system sits above the brain stem and below the cerebral cortex. Two of the major structures of this system are the

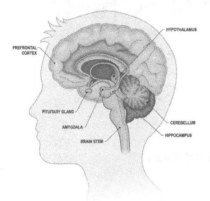

hippocampus (stores memories and connects them to sensations) and the amygdala (helps keeps us safe and is where our emotions develop). Also engaged in the limbic emotional system are the thalamus (relays sensory information, including vision, taste, touch, and balance to the cortex), hypothalamus (regulates emotions, sleep, behavior, and pain), and basal ganglia (controls motor learning, emotional behaviors, and habit formation).

Then you have the frontal lobe, which is the top layer and includes the cerebral cortex. This is where our executive functioning and critical-thinking skills develop. Mixed in here are our auditory and visual senses and our balance—all those things that we're learning to do. Now, if a child is being raised in a home where there's love, good communication, and safety, and the parents are staying attuned to the child's needs and abilities, those neurological pathways that communicate with all areas of our brain will connect and develop as they're supposed to. In that environment, a child develops what is known as a secure attachment, and how a child attaches to their caregiver sets the foundation for their development.

The significant connection between a child's level of attachment to their caregiver and their healthy development was first theorized in 1970 by psychologist Mary Ainsworth. She is best known for the development of her strange situation classification (SSC), which identified three main styles of attachment:

- Secure attachment

- Ambivalent-insecure attachment

- Avoidant-insecure attachment[5]

In 1986, researchers Main and Solomon identified a fourth attachment style:

- Disorganized-insecure attachment[6]

In Ainsworth's SSC, the child (between the ages of twelve and eighteen months) is observed behind a two-way mirror when their mother is in the room with them, when their mother leaves the room and the child is left alone, and when the mother returns. The experiment also observes a child when a stranger enters the room while the child is alone and when the mother returns to the room. Below is a chart displaying the behaviors in each scenario and the category of attachment the behaviors fall under.

In Main and Solomon's disorganized-insecure attachment theory, a child becomes unsure about their attachment to their caregiver and

---

5   Saul Mcleod, "Mary Ainsworth: Strange Situation Experiment & Attachment Theory," updated March 8, 2023, https://www.simplypsychology.org/mary-ainsworth. html#:~:text=The%20Strange%20Situation%20%7C%20Attachment%20 Styles&text=The%20strange%20situation%20is%20a,of%20nine%20and%2018%20 months.

6   Kendra Cherry, "The Different Types of Attachment Styles," Very Well Mind, updated May 26, 2022, https://www.verywellmind.com/attachment-styles-2795344#:~:text=Based%20on%20these%20observations%2C%20 Ainsworth,known%20as%20disorganized%2Dinsecure%20attachment.

	SECURE	RESISTANT	AVOIDANT
SEPARATION ANXIETY	Distressed when mother leaves	Intense distress when the mother leaves	No sign of distress when the mother leaves
STRANGER ANXIETY	Avoidant of stranger when alone, but friendly when the mother is present	The infant avoids the stranger— shows fear of the stranger	The infant is okay with the stranger and plays normally when the stranger is present
REUNION BEHAVIOR	Positive and happy when the mother returns	The infant approaches the mother, but resists contact, may even push her away	The infant shows little interest when the mother returns
OTHER	Uses the mother as a safe base to explore their environment	The infant cries more and explores less than the other two types	The mother and stranger are able to comfort the infant equally well

These types of insecure attachments are formed if a child is in a home where there is ongoing stress, which could include the child experiencing the anxious and fearful energy of their loving parent or the child who is being physically or emotionally abused by their parent. They will not learn to trust or be curious about their environment, and those neuropathways will not connect as they should. Why? Because the child's need to be on heightened alert will keep the brain focused on overdeveloping their fight, flight, or freeze response in the amygdala, making it impossible to form a healthy foundational attachment to their caregiver and decreasing the brain's ability to develop other critical areas.

Children who live in extreme stress between the ages of birth to three tend to have language, balance, and emotional deregulation issues—the pathways that should have been created couldn't happen because the body was being constantly flooded with cortisol and adrenaline in response to the cycle of stress the child is feeling. The more repetition when learning language, finding our balance, or recognizing our emotions and learning

> A child becomes unsure about their attachment to their caregiver and may display a mixture of avoidant and resistant behavior.

how to regulate them, the bigger that neuropathway gets and the better we get at what we are trying to do.

Language is just one example of what we learn through continuous exposure that makes meaningful and memorable connections. If you've ever taught a child what a fire truck is, you might have started by pointing to one in a book, saying "fire truck," and imitating its sound. Then when you and your child saw a real fire truck, you repeated the same three steps of pointing, saying the word, and making the sound, and every time your child attempted to say the word and make the sound, you praised them—"You did it!" And that's how we learn *everything* through repetition that builds connection until we have a ten-lane highway of connections. In a home ruled by dependency-, fear-, and reward-based parenting, the ten-lane highway of connections a child builds is "The world is not safe" or "You are not capable, so I have to do everything for you" or "You will never be good enough."

These messages can be sent by loving and well-meaning parents who believe their child is the greatest, but if the message they are unintentionally sending is "I have to do this for you because you aren't capable and the world is too dangerous," they'll develop an abundance of anxiety and a lack of self-confidence—the opposite of what we want for our children.

TAKE A MOMENT

Make a list of the first ten words that come to mind when describing your child and put the list aside for now.

Loosening the Grip: Developing Balance

Meet "Sam," a two-year-old toddler who was referred for therapy by his preschool teacher because of developmental concerns. His mother insisted on carrying him almost everywhere because she was so concerned about him falling. Sam was allowed to walk around limited areas of the house—all the furniture in the house was padded—but he was not allowed to learn how to climb up or down stairs, and when they went anywhere in public, Sam had to be in a stroller or carried. When Sam entered preschool, Mom tried to insist that the teachers carry him around. Limiting his opportunity to learn how to walk, run, and climb was impacting Sam's motor development and balance as well as his security and self-confidence. As a result, Sam was not able to move with the same balance, agility, and strength that his peers were, and he was becoming highly fearful of most situations. In addition, having been conditioned to always be carried, he had begun to demand it constantly.

When a two-year-old is referred for therapy, it's not usually the child who needs the help; it's the parents. This is not about placing blame; Mom deeply loved and cared for her son. This is about recognizing our role as parents in our child's development and appreciating the tremendous impact, both positive and negative, that we can consciously and unconsciously have on our child's well-being.

IDENTIFYING THE SOURCE

After meeting with the parents a couple of times, a few things became evident.

1. The parents had very different ideas of parenting.

2. Dad was highly uninvolved.

3. Mom was uberprotective.

This is when self-reflection comes in to help the parents determine why they are parenting the way they are parenting. In Sam's case, his dad was too far on the uninvolved end of the spectrum because he himself had been raised by parents whose parenting style was pretty hands-off. Sam's mom had a very traumatic childhood that had ingrained her with fear and was supercharging her belief that she needed to constantly protect her son.

While Sam needed to be taught self-confidence in his own ability to function in his world, Mom and Dad needed couples counseling and Mom needed trauma counseling so they could develop the parenting tools they needed to help Sam gain age-appropriate autonomy.

DOING THE WORK

The first step was helping Mom address her fear that was depriving Sam of a healthy development. For that, we needed to identify her worst-case scenario and work on decatastrophizing it. I asked her what her biggest fear about letting Sam walk was. Her fear was that he could fall and break his neck.

"OK, let's look at that. What if there's an accident and Sam has broken his neck. Now what happens?"

Mom immediately began to cry. I reminded her that we were just going to walk through an imaginary scenario. In her worst-case scenario, Sam falls and dies. From there, over many months, we walked through what would happen if Sam fell and died. Her initial response was that she would kill herself. Over time, she came to see that although it would be excruciatingly painful, she would survive.

Eventually, we got to a point where she could envision where she might be in six months after Sam's death. "I'd still be sad, but I'd have to start functioning because I'd have to have a job, I'd have responsibilities."

"Where do you see yourself in a year?" I asked.

Mom hoped that she might be pregnant and that she would make sure she never allowed her child to be unsafe. And we would start the decatastrophizing process again. Eventually, we hit on Mom's real fear: that if anything bad happened to her child, it would be her fault. And so we worked through that scenario.

"OK, you are being blamed for Sam's accident. You're being checked in by child protection, and you could go to jail. People think you're a horrible mother. Now what?" I asked her.

"But I'm not a horrible mother," she said.

"Why not?" I asked.

And she went on to list all the good and caring ways she took care of Sam. She agreed that she knew the truth about what kind of mother she was—she was a good one. And we were able to get to the point that she also agreed that the chances of Sam falling and breaking his neck by walking was almost impossible. It was at that point we could talk about the importance of developing Sam's motor skills and self-confidence.

Through Mom's work on addressing her own fears and Dad learning to become a more connected dad and husband, the family began to move to solid ground, and Sam began to gradually build the autonomy he deserved.

BUILDING EMOTIONAL RESILIENCE

We've all been in those situations when we experienced a flash of anger but the appropriate response to the situation required us to remain calm and polite. Perhaps it was after a long day at work, and you made a quick stop at the grocery store to pick up a couple of things you needed for dinner. As you get in the "ten or fewer items" checkout line, you realize the person in front of you has an overflowing carriage. "This line is for ten items," you mumble under your breath, frustrated that you will now be late getting home, and your basket of eight items suddenly feels heavier. What do you do? Do you unleash all your frustrations and loudly berate the rule breaker in front of you? Do you politely tell the person that they are in the wrong line and direct them to the appropriate one? What if they respond, "I'm already in line. I'm not moving." Then you loudly berate them, right? Or maybe your sense of reasoning kicks in, and you decide the best option is to take a deep breath and choose not to let this slight delay ruin your entire evening.

Even for the emotionally regulated adult, this simple scenario can require a lot of processing to take place in a short amount of time—processing that we may not even realize is happening. While our innate temperament plays a role in our natural ability to regulate our emotions, we need help to fully develop our ability to respond appropriately to situations despite our emotions. Let's jump back into the science of our child's development to help us figure out how to teach our children to control their emotions and make the best decisions even when we are not around.

> We need help to fully develop our ability to respond appropriately to situations despite our emotions.

In their book *The Whole-Brain Child*, Dr. Daniel Siegel and Dr. Tina Payne Bryson explain how to integrate what they refer to as the "upstairs" and "downstairs" of our brain to promote healthy emotional regulation. The downstairs of our brain is the lower half we discussed previously, which includes the brain stem and our limbic region. Together, the downstairs includes our basic functions, innate reactions, and strong emotions: all instinctual, involuntary responses to ensure our basic survival. Our upstairs brain involves the far more sophisticated and complex cerebral cortex. This is where are critical thinking and executive functioning develops. This is the part of the brain that talks us into making rational choices and appropriate reactions when all we want to do is scream, "I want it and I want it now!"

Before we can begin to help our child engage their upstairs brain with their downstairs brain, Siegel and Payne Bryson make clear that we must set realistic expectations based on basic developmental facts.

1. The downstairs brain is well developed at birth.

2. The upstairs brain isn't fully developed until our midtwenties.

Our midtwenties! That explains a lot about how teenagers at times seem to regress in their ability to reason. Here's what's happening there: pruning.

USE IT OR LOSE IT

Around the age of eleven, our brain does this thing called *pruning*, at which time the neuron connections we haven't been accessing go off-line. The brain does this to make room for new, more complex structures that we need to continue our development. While pruning is intended to get rid of connections our brain doesn't need, it will shut down pathways that we *do* need simply because we aren't using them. Those connections become dormant until we begin to intentionally tap back into them. It's like hiking down a cleared, well-marked path, and then over to your right you see what kind of looks like it was a path, but there's a lot of overgrowth happening and no visible track marks. That path is like the brain's pathway that has gone off-line. And just like the hiking path, you can clear the debris that's developed in your neuropathways and begin to use them again.

Parents play a crucial role in keeping their children's pathways open and engaged—or becoming dormant. If parents make all their children's decisions for them, never let them fail and recover, never hold them accountable, the pathways to developing those skills will shut down.

Here's an example of what I am talking about. I walked into a middle school a couple of weeks ago, and on the counter in the main office was a pile of student's paraphernalia: textbooks, notebooks, instruments, cleats, hats, so much stuff. I asked the staff what it all was for, and I was shocked when she told me these were all things the students had forgotten to bring with them this morning and that their parents had all been coming in and dropping off.

I was dumbfounded. "Don't most of the parents work?" I asked.

"Yes," she said, "but when their child calls, they bring them whatever it was they forgot at home."

I couldn't help thinking that these kids were being set up. If at eleven, twelve, thirteen years of age they were being taught to believe that if they forgot something, someone would magically bring it to them, how would they ever learn to be responsible for themselves? I could see their neuropathways closing. When were their parents going to finally respond to their call about a forgotten item with, "I'm so sorry that you forgot your ____; sounds like it's going to make your day a bit challenging, but I know you'll get through it"? You can still empathize with them, but you don't need to (and shouldn't) rescue them at every turn. If you do, they will never learn to rescue themselves when challenged, or worse yet, they will never build the skills to prevent them from needing to be constantly rescued. Those pathways will be "pruned" away because of lack of use. You wouldn't intentionally let your children's muscles atrophy—don't let their brain atrophy either!

Based on the regularity and volume of what I've seen—and I know this happens in high schools, too, and sometimes even in college—this is not isolated to a few parents, and it's not just about bringing forgotten items to school. It's about today's prevailing mindset that parents should cater to their child's every need, ensuring that they never feel frustrated or at risk of failing. It has become an unhealthy norm, and it's hurting our children. Life is about challenges. Life is about difficulty. Life is about figuring those things out, because when life is going great, it's pretty simple to live. But when it's not and an individual hasn't developed any tools or abilities to cope, they will not be able to navigate life's frustrations and risks in a healthy way.

It's our responsibility as parents to provide our children the tools and resources to develop the skills of and connection to their upstairs brain. It's important to also provide grace during the moments when their brain just isn't developed enough to sustain those skills. Even if they "got it" yesterday, it doesn't mean they will "get it" next Monday.

Even though at six years old a child may be able to tell you the rules, it doesn't mean they are always capable of following them.

So how can parents help develop and integrate their child's upstairs brain in a healthy way? *The Whole-Brain Child* offers three strategies:

1. **Engage, don't enrage: appealing to the upstairs brain.**

   We all have bad moods and moments of anger, but how we deal with those feelings and help our children deal with them is key to our and their emotional health. Let's say your child comes home from school and suddenly starts yelling and throwing down their backpack. Clearly, something is going on, but you have no idea what. Depending on your own mood at the time, your reaction may be to raise your voice and demand to know what all the yelling is about. That response will enrage rather than engage your child.

   Your role is to remain calm and help them de-escalate. You can do that by acknowledging they're upset. "Wow, you seem pretty upset. Do you want to talk about it?" If they don't want to talk, suggest you get them a snack. Ask them what they would like to eat or drink, and encourage them to take a seat while you get it ready.

   When I worked in crisis intervention, I called this *sandwich therapy*. By the time I was seeing someone on a crisis call in the ER, they would have been there three to four hours. My job was to help them move out of the back part of the brain where their fight, flight, or flee response was taking over and move them into their upstairs brain to engage their critical-thinking skills. One of the first things I'd say is, "You hungry? Can I get you something to eat or drink?" They would say yes, and with that new focus and attention, their whole demeanor would change.

Once you've prompted your child to engage their upstairs brain, the communication lines open back up. They may still need you to just sit quietly with them for a bit, but as long as they are calm, they will be able to begin processing their feelings and the situation that upset them.

2. Use it or lose it: exercising the upstairs brain.

Training your brain to emotionally regulate: the ability to return to a calm state and think critically. If you don't exercise your muscles, they will atrophy. If you don't exercise your critical-thinking skills, those neuropathways will close down. This means you have to let your child figure things out. If you rush in every time to make sure they never get frustrated, they will never learn to deal with frustration. Don't eliminate the opportunity for them to experience their feelings or dismiss them when they do express them. Help them learn how to work through them.

3. Move it or lose it: moving the body to avoid losing the mind.

We were evolved to wake up in the morning, work throughout the daylight, and then return to whatever "home" was at dusk to eat and sleep. We lived off the land. We worked hard and were in constant motion. That motion released feel-good hormones like dopamine, serotonin, endorphins, and oxytocin. In today's world, we don't activate our feel-good hormones enough because we aren't moving enough!

When we feel down or are experiencing depression, the last thing we want to do is get ourselves moving, but that is exactly the remedy we need. Even if it's just fifteen minutes a day, make the time to exercise your body to avoid losing your mind.

Is My Child Showing Signs of Hypervigilant Parenting?

Do your friends' children or your child's friends participate in activities, chores, responsibilities that your child doesn't do at that age? Are they allowed to do things that you don't allow your child to do at that age? Is your child fearful of unfamiliar people and circumstances? Are they afraid of failing, so they don't bother trying new things? Is your child constantly expecting you to rescue them? Is your ten-year-old still throwing tantrums like a two-year-old when they don't get their way?

If the answer is yes to any of these, you may be practicing hypervigilant parenting, and your child's development may be suffering as a result. Here are some common traits of children being parented through dependency-, fear-, and reward-based needs: anxious, fearful, entitled, dependent, easily frustrated, low self-confidence, and stressed.

While the negative impact of hypervigilant parenting is not great news, there is good news. If you are in some way impeding your child's development toward becoming a fully functioning, independent adult, you also have the power to shift gears and begin to nurture and empower their healthy development instead.

Reflection:

- *Take out the list you made of ten words that describe your child. How many of them are signs of your dependency-, fear-, or reward-based needs, like anxious, fearful, entitled, dependent, easily frustrated, low self-confidence, and stressed?*

- *Think about the situations in which your child exhibits these traits and how you address them.*

- *Consider whether your expectations of your child are appropriate. If they are too low or too high, what steps could you to adjust those expectations appropriately?*

- *Complete the online parenting style assessment (you'll find a QR code at the back of this book).*

CHAPTER 3

The Good News

♥

If you're the root cause, you also have the power to be the solution.

—LISA K. ANDERSON

When my daughter was three, I asked her to clean her whole room by herself. She did not. I was in a bad mood, and I went in, grabbed one of her plastic chairs, slammed it to the ground (breaking it), and said, "You start cleaning up your fucking room." I looked at her, and in her eyes were these big tears. I saw her fear, and I remembered the fear I had when my mom would come into my room that way. That was the first time I went to a counselor for parenting help.

That was not a proud parent moment for me, but as difficult as it is to share, it's important that I do, because that was the moment that set me on my path to where I am today: a better parent for my daughter and a guide for other parents who want to do better, to be better parents for their children.

So how did I magically become a perfect parent? I didn't. There is no magic. There is no perfect parent. My path to being a better, more attuned parent (and now grandparent) was not an easy road, and I continue to stumble along, making improvements to how I parent while simultaneously making new mistakes. Remember the balance scale from chapter 1? Well, over time, I've swung back and forth.

When my daughter was six, the advisors at her school expressed concern that she had ADHD. I took her to a psychologist who, after months of testing, diagnosed her with "BRAT syndrome." It took me a minute to realize what he meant. He was saying that my daughter was a brat. My defenses immediately went up. "What do you mean my daughter is a brat?" I demanded.

"I've never seen you say no to your child in the six months you've both been coming here."

"Well, there's been no reason to say no to her."

"Oh, there've been many reasons she should have been told no," he replied.

Then he started listing them all off, and I was like, "Oh, my daughter is a brat."

I went home and asked my husband, "Do you think that I've made our daughter into a brat?"

"Yes," was his immediate reply.

I was taken aback. "What do you mean?"

"Any time I try to discipline her or tell her no, you immediately undermine me or jump in and tell me that that's not how we're going to do it. So, yes. You have made her into a brat."

That night I put in the video tape the psychologist gave me called *1, 2, 3 Magic*. I started to reflect on past experiences in a new light— like the time my daughter's preschool teacher told me that when they tried to tell her she had to pick up her toys, she took her arm out and walked all along the shelf and knocked every toy off. It just dawned on me now that she wasn't trying to share a cute anecdote; she was trying to tell me there was a problem. In that moment, I realized that I was the problem and that if I didn't change my way of thinking and shift my focus from what I needed to what my daughter needed, I was going to create a little monster.

That's a tough pill to swallow for any parent. But once you've had the courage to do it, you realize you also have the power to change and create a better outcome for you and your child.

To develop your power to change, you must first be willing to look at the root causes of why you are parenting that way. Is it driven by fear, guilt, too much ego, lack of confidence, past trauma? Is it simply just what you know without giving thought to whether it's healthy for you or your child?

We know children need guidance, discipline, and emotional support to build healthy neuropathways and connect their downstairs brain

> Just like there are many ways to parent, there are many reasons why we parent the way we do.

with their upstairs brain, so why is it sometimes hard for loving parents to do that? Just like there are many ways to parent, there are many reasons why we parent the way we do. Let's look at a few of those reasons.

Generational Shifts and Their Influence on Parenting

Each generation develops how they parent according to the current social and economic pressures and in response to the way that they were raised by previous generations. Changing tides of generational parenting is like a pendulum that often overcorrects, swinging too far in one direction to "fix" the previous direction. This is called the *slingshot effect*, and those swings are evident when you look at changes in parenting styles across generations. While generational parenting is not the only factor of how someone parents, or even the primary factor, I believe it has a fair measure of influence. Here are popular generalizations about four different generations that have impacted how we look at childrearing.

SILENT GENERATION (BORN BETWEEN 1928 AND 1945)

My parents were from the silent generation, a generation of children who had been traumatized by being raised during the Great Depression and World War II. They grew up without the stability of many necessities, and when they became parents, they indulged their children in material things. But that is where their indulgence stopped. They did not tend to their children's emotional needs, holding firm to their belief that "children should be seen but not heard" and to that old adage "Spare the rod, spoil the child."

BABY BOOMERS (BORN BETWEEN 1946 AND 1964)

Having been given material abundances in childhood, boomers grew up to be entitled and self-involved—often titled the "narcissistic generation." Growing up during the Vietnam War and the Civil Rights Movement, boomers found their voices and demanded changes. Wealth for the middle generation expanded, college and careers were prioritized, two working parents became the norm, and so did the baby boomers' self-indulgence. Children were often left home alone after school, and their emotional needs were often ignored. Boomers raised what are known as latchkey kids, who were often left without adult supervision.

GEN X (BORN BETWEEN 1965 AND 1980)

Because Gen Xers grew up feeling emotionally neglected by their parents, who were out building *their* careers and living *their* lives, when they became parents they were hell bent on making sure they emotionally attended to their children. When Gen Xers lost as children, there was nobody there to help them with those emotions. To fix that problem, there would be no losers in their children's world because everyone would be declared a winner!

Every child received trophies for simply being there and offering some level of participation. The children who put in the effort to make the win happen felt cheated, and the ones who contributed little felt embarrassed and guilty for receiving equal accolades. The result? Effort was no longer needed to win, and the Gen Xers' children (the millennials) grew up believing that they were entitled to everything regardless of how little effort they put in to get it. The emotional needs of millennials, just like their parents, remained unmet, leaving them with no skills or tolerance to deal with life's inevitable frustrations and disappointments.

MILLENNIALS (BORN BETWEEN 1981 AND 1996)

Millennials are the first generation to grow up with access to computers and cell phones—a world of knowledge and communication at their fingertips. They are the first generation to parent in the age of unrelenting social media. They have been described as confident and accepting but also entitled and narcissistic.

When the millennials became parents, they saw the flaw in "Everyone gets a trophy" and doubled down on attuning to their child's feelings and helping them work through those feelings. A popular methodology used by this generation is called *gentle parenting*. When done correctly, this method can help parents provide their children the tools needed to fully develop their executive functioning and critical-thinking skills, helping them to connect the dots between their emotions and how to regulate them.

But like every parenting philosophy out there, there is no one-size-fits-all, and there is always opportunity for misinterpretation. I have begun to see the consequences of misinterpreting gentle parenting with Gen Z children, who are being raised by millennials. The result is *permissive parenting*. The example I gave of parents regularly adapting their schedule to rush their children's forgotten items to school is just one example of parents not holding their children accountable, not encouraging or allowing them to learn to be responsible and face the natural consequences when they choose not to be.

I also see schools doing away with grades or allowing students to redo assignments and tests as many times as they need to pass. What's the motivation for the student to put in the effort the first time they do the assignment or take the test, or the second time or the third time, when there's always another chance? When those students get to college and are handed a failing grade, they'll assume they can just redo it, and they will be wrong. This policy is doing a huge disservice to our children. They're not preparing the college-bound or work-bound student for reality. When a young adult enters the workforce and they make mistakes, they'll be in for a shock when their boss doesn't share their "What's the big deal? I'll just redo it" mindset. Life isn't one redo after another. What professional providing a service would you be OK with having the redo mindset? Hairdresser, chef, firefighter? What about your surgeon? Parents need to help their children develop skills for the long game, not just what feels safe and comfortable in the moment.

The Influence of Emotions

Just as a child's behaviors are the tip of an iceberg, so are the parents'.

Beneath our reactions are our feelings, and beneath those are the many influencers of those feelings. Behaviors that parents exhibit toward children are often about meeting their own emotional needs rather than their children's.

Parents are often (unconsciously) guided by fear, guilt, and societal pressures rather than their child's developmental needs.

Let's see how those emotions, if not acknowledged and regulated in the parent, affect the child.

Guilt and fear are the top two emotions I hear from parents when talking about why they interact with their child the way they do. Then anger and disappointment creep in. Like peeling an onion,

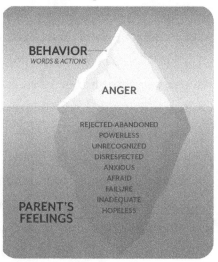

emotions have many layers underneath that can lead to our expressions of guilt, fear, and anger. For our purposes here, I'm going to focus on those three emotions: how and why they show up, and best practices to regulate and reframe those emotions.

GUILT

No one is immune to guilt, and yes, sometimes it drives us to do (or not do) things. Occasionally letting your child have an extra hour of gaming because you feel guilty for dragging them around on errands all day is not the end of the world. Parenting based on a foundation of guilt—that is a significant problem. A problem that fills an unhealthy need for the parent and neglects the child's needs.

Loosening the Grip: Making the Connection

Meet "Claire," a five-year-old girl who was finding the transition to kindergarten challenging. Claire refused to do anything she didn't want to do and would go as far as throw her work on the floor and tell her teacher to pick it up. Claire wanted what she wanted when she wanted it and expected everyone to respond quickly to her demands. Claire was having behavioral issues that needed to be fixed. But first we needed to figure out the *why* of her behaviors before we could develop the *how* to help her change them.

Claire had two older brothers, and Mom believed that daughters should be treated as special. So she doted on Claire and provided her everything she needed and wanted without Claire having to ask for it. While the boys were expected to pick up after themselves and have some responsibilities around the house, Claire was not. Mom picked up after Claire and provided for Claire. When Claire developed a voice, she began to make demands. By five, Claire would sit on the couch and tell her mother to bring her breakfast, a drink, whatever it was she wanted, and Mom would. When Mom tried to set some expectations and refused to cater to her daughter, Claire would threaten to tell her father, and Mom didn't want Dad to think she was not treating their daughter right, so she would give in.

When you look at Claire's environment, it's clear that Mom had unintentionally taught her daughter to be irresponsible, demanding, and disrespectful. Now, due to changing circumstances, it suddenly needed to stop so she could be successful in kindergarten and Mom could provide the family's new baby with the attention she needed.

Why did this happen?

Mom's ingrained belief that daughters needed to be treated as special filled her with guilt whenever she felt she failed to meet that expectation. Mom also felt guilty because Claire was sometimes picked on by her brothers, and she felt the need to compensate for that. Add to that a marriage that was not fulfilling her emotional needs, and sometimes it was just hard for her to get out of her own way.

DOING THE WORK

The process to "fix" Claire's behavior required a lot of work, including working on her parents' marriage, helping Mom understand that her expectations for her daughter were unrealistic and that she needed to set a higher bar for Claire without feeling guilty about it, and then helping Claire strengthen the connection between her upstairs and downstairs brain to develop her ability to reason, regulate her emotions, and build confidence in what she was capable of doing for herself.

PARENTING STEPS

The first step was helping Mom figure out where her guilt came from. Not surprisingly, she had a very critical mother and never felt like she could make her happy, which manifested into the belief that she couldn't make "females" happy, and so she catered to her daughter.

Once the source of her guilt was identified, we did an exercise where I would say the statement "I feel guilty when …" and she would fill in the blank. I would choose different topics around being a mother, wife, and daughter.

Next, Claire's mom learned to set boundaries with her own mother and with Claire. This all took a lot of time, commitment, and practice on Mom's part. Mom was encouraged to and did participate in a moms' group to help get some needed adult interaction.

Claire had areas to work on, too, and she and I practiced tools she could use and identified resources to help her regulate her emotions. It was a long process but one that did improve over time. One day, Claire came in with a picture to show me.

"What is this?" I asked.

"It's a picture of my clothes that I put away by myself."

"Doesn't that feel good to take care of your own things?" I asked.

"Yes," she said with a smile, "and I set the table now too!"

She then went on to confess that she had dropped a fork one day and put it back on the table, making me swear that I wouldn't tell her mom.

We laughed, and I asked, "What could you do if you drop a fork again?"

She smiled and said, "I'll get a clean one."

FEAR

While guilt is often the first emotion I hear parents express, once we dig just below the surface of their guilt, we discover fear is the driving force. I have observed parents who raise their children through fear. Not the authoritarian fear that baby boomers were raised with but rather parents making decisions about how to parent based on their own fears and sometimes instilling those fears in their children.

I worked with a nine-year-old girl who was fearful of just about everything: getting on the bus, going to the bathroom by herself at school, hanging out at her friends' houses, public spaces. This child had been previously diagnosed with social anxiety disorder, generalized anxiety disorder, panic disorder, agoraphobia, you name it. By the fifth session, she was finally comfortable enough with me that she was OK with her mom staying in the waiting room while she and I talked. So I got out the toys, and we started playing and talking. It went something like this:

Me: "How come you're afraid to get on the bus?"

Child: "Well, Mom reminds me all the time that buses don't have seat buckles. And because there's no seat buckles, if we have an accident, I could die on that bus."

Me: "Why is Mom reminding you of that?"

Child: "So that if I'm sitting there, I remember to make sure that I'm being aware that the bus could have an accident and that I'm not goofing and playing around. I need to stay aware of that."

Me: "So, tell me, why are *you* afraid?"

Over weeks of talking with this child in this way, there was a clear connection between her fears and what Mom has told her to be afraid of. It was a constant statement: "Well, Mom said …" After four weeks of this, I met with Mom and Dad alone.

I explained to them that, unfortunately, their daughter did have some real anxiety and that there is a genetic component to anxiety, but in their daughter's case, it was a behavior that she had been taught.

They looked at each other and then at me and asked, "Who's teaching her that?"

I started naming all the things that Mom, according to her daughter, was afraid of, parroting back to her how she tells her daughter to always be alert and all the ways harm could come to her.

"Doesn't that sound frightening?" I asked.

She agreed it did but that that was not her intention. I explained that that was how her daughter was hearing it and it was making her afraid of everything, including being away from her mother for any period of time. Fortunately, the relationship between Mom and Dad was strong. Mom had had an abusive upbringing that had created her fears and an overriding need to keep her child safe at all costs. Dad was caught in a balancing act between supporting his wife's fears and not overprotecting his daughter.

In these cases of parenting driven by fear-based needs, the truth is the child is made less safe because they've never been allowed to learn how to take care of themselves. Once both parents were able to recognize their role in their daughter's hyperfears, we had a lot of undoing to do. Mom worked through her own trauma issues with another therapist, and the parents and I worked together to very gradually provide their daughter opportunities to try new things. This was a case where the child's anxiety symptoms were so intense that a low dose of medication was needed for her to be able to work through the therapy. By the end of a year, she was much more relaxed and more confident, and so were Mom and Dad.

> In these cases of parenting driven by fear-based needs, the truth is the child is made less safe because they've never been allowed to learn how to take care of themselves.

The fears that most parents have for their children are physical: they fear their child will be the victim of violence or hurt in some other way. There is this idea that "if my child is outside of my vision, I can't keep him or her safe." These fears are encouraged by the news and how statistics surrounding dangers are relayed. Terms like *likelihood* and *prevalence* are often used, even when they are not true descriptors. As a result, parents are allowing fear to drive how much they let their children do, even if those fears are unfounded.

ANGER

There are so many emotions that are thrown into the mix in addition to guilt, fear, and anger—sadness, disappointment, and frustration, to name a few—and not everyone's emotions peel back in the same order. I had one dad who would frequently express anger when his daughter didn't do as well in school as he thought she could. Even if she got an A-minus, he would be angry that she didn't put in a bit more effort to get an A-plus when he knew she was capable of doing so. His daughter is gifted and could have gotten A-pluses across the board, but sometimes, an A-minus or even a B was good enough for her. The dad really struggled with getting past the "But she could have done better" thought process.

Once we dug a little deeper and I pushed him to identify why this made him so angry, his response was, "I don't want her to be a failure like me." This dad was not a failure. He had overcome the challenges of unsupportive parents and undiagnosed ADHD to become a loving and supportive dad and husband and a successful business owner. And still those original feelings of disappointment and failure were defining his view of himself and showing up as anger. Once he was able to identify the source, we were able to work on reframing his view of himself as a failure.

INFLUENCES OF SOCIETAL PRESSURE

I brought my three-year-old granddaughter to the park one day with a mop of messy hair and chocolate ice cream still on her face, because she wouldn't let me wash her face or comb her hair. I got more than a few judging looks, but I didn't care. We were having fun, and when we got home, I put her in the tub and all was good.

Would you take your child out like this? Why or why not?

Societal pressure is not new, not created by the advent of social media. People have always judged, and people have always felt judged. What social media has done is intensify the pressure a hundredfold. For some, I imagine it feels even greater than that. For some, it can feel like piranhas are lurking around every corner waiting for them to slip up. I wouldn't be surprised if someone snapped a picture of my granddaughter that day and posted it with a hypercritical comment.

Today's in-your-face societal pressure is a challenge to navigate, to be sure, but at some point, parents must develop the confidence to just stop worrying about it.

I've had parents come in my office with their child and say, "Oh my gosh, I'm so embarrassed about what they're wearing. They just wouldn't listen to me, and then we had to get going." Their child is standing right there! So here's this six-year-old who is really proud of what they chose, and they like it and think they look good, and then their parents berate them—in front of others, no less. That child's self-esteem just took a huge hit.

Parents who are hypercritical of their children are generally hypercritical of themselves, and they see their children's looks, actions, etc. as a reflection on them. Parents feel pressure to make sure their kids have what the other kids have—and today, those comparisons are constantly made because everyone has posted what they have on Facebook, Instagram, TikTok, you name it. I urge parents to not buy into it. And if you are, be honest about why you're buying into it. Why is it so important that others approve of what you or your family look like, have, or do?

> **TAKE A MOMENT**
>
> For the next forty-eight hours, pay attention to when you feel the need to criticize your child. Write down those instances, and put the list aside for now.

It's not always easy to take an honest assessment of how we parent. It's even tougher to acknowledge the mistakes we've made. But the good news is you have the power to be the solution, to find the right balance of guidance and freedom for your child.

Reflections

- *Take out the list of your top three fears for your child, and be honest with yourself about whether they are based in reality or are fears you grew up with and are simply passing on. If you believe they are based in reality, do some fact-based research to prove (or disprove) their validity.*

- *Take out the list of times when you felt the need to correct, criticize, or rescue your child. Step back and look at each of those situations as an objective observer, and identify what was driving you to take those actions. Were those reasons appropriate to the situation or driven by your own emotions?*

- *Practice recognizing those situations and taking a moment to step out of your own emotions before engaging with your child.*

CHAPTER 4

Guidance and Freedom: Finding the Right Balance for Your Child

Don't worry that children never listen to you; worry that they are always watching you.

—ROBERT FULGHUM

Teachers often have a front-row seat to the imbalance hypervigilant parenting can have on their students—children who are unable to independently think through how to solve a problem or children who have a meltdown if they make even the smallest of mistakes. Sometimes, teachers also have the opportunity to observe hypervigilant parenting in action.

Teacher and TikToker Anita Bond shares one such experience in which she observed two fifth-grade girls and their moms working on the girls' homework together—well, what she really observed was the moms doing their daughters' homework.[7]

---

7   Anita Bond (@a.bond.teach), TikTok, September 28, 2022, https://www.tiktok.com/@a.bond.teach/video/7148474301644115246?_r=1&_t=8WGYuZEWqSM&is_from_webapp=v1&item_id=7148474301644115246.

"One mom was googling what a quotient is. Both moms had their fingers on their kids' papers telling them exactly what to do step by step. 'Now subtract this. OK, now you want this over here. Now take this piece of paper and put it in your math folder.' I not once watched one of those two girls have to make an independent decision about what happens next, what they need next, what the next step is, how to solve the problem. They didn't have to do it once. Their parents told them exactly what to do next for forty-five minutes."

Bond goes on to point out the negative impact for these fifth-grade students:

- Any grade the girls receive for their homework will be overstated as a result of their moms' "support."

- Maybe the students did know how to do the math problems, but there's no way of knowing since they were not given an opportunity to even try to figure them out.

- Homework is meant to provide students the opportunity to practice what they learned in the classroom; these girls did not get any of that.

"But here's the tricky and very, very important part, those girls are going to go back to school, and they are going to expect that level of support with every tricky problem that they have … so when we're trying to encourage problem solving, trying to encourage independent thinking, trying to encourage students to use their resources to execute a process on their own, that same skill development is not happening at home."

By providing this level of "support," parents are robbing their children of any opportunity to develop any real thinking skill, a skill that will not suddenly appear when they are adults. So if we are not teaching it to them now, then when?

Children need guidance; no one is debating that. But equally important in their development into adulthood is their freedom to learn, and in order to learn, we must be allowed to fail. Failing is not losing. Failing is learning. It's trying. It's persevering. It's building capacity to overcome. All these skills build self-confidence. When you try something new and you get it right on the first attempt, it feels pretty good, right? What about when you don't get it right the first time and you try again, and it still doesn't work? You look at the problem and try to solve it another way. Still, you can't seem to figure it out. On the fourth attempt, you get creative, and you work at it some more, and you solve it! How much more triumphant do you feel when you figure it out on your fourth attempt than you did on your first? How much deeper did you engage your brain with each attempt?

Do we want to have to try everything four or more times to get it right? Of course not, but if we want to regularly engage and develop our brains, we sometimes *need* to fail and try, fail and try, and fail and try again.

Today, children's threshold of tolerance for frustration or disappointment, of not getting it the first time, is incredibly low. So often, parents will tell me, "I don't know why she's like this. If she can't figure out a homework problem immediately, she'll put her pencil down and start crying and saying she's a loser."

I'll ask them what they do when their child does that. "Well, she's crying and feeling so bad about herself that I just do it for her." And just like that, the child's opportunity to build confidence in their ability to solve a problem or emotionally cope with a challenge is gone. It's hard to watch our children struggle and cry. It's natural for us parents to want to "fix" everything for our children. But in the end, it is our children who suffer for those "fixes" that, in the moment, make us feel better.

When children have all their problems solved for them, when every decision is made for them, when they are used to being told what to do, when they have not developed some understanding of how to assess the risk versus the reward of a situation, they will be unprepared to make the life-altering decisions that they will inevitably face when their parents are not there. Your fifteen-year-old son's friend tells him to hop in the car and go for a ride with them. The driver is intoxicated. Your son doesn't have the ability to critically think about his options and he doesn't have the self-confidence to stand against even the slightest peer pressure. He certainly cannot tolerate being seen as a loser. He gets in the car.

No parent sets out to intentionally create that scenario, and fortunately there are methods and resources that can assist parents in finding the balance between guidance and freedom that provides a loving and safe environment that encourages a child's age-appropriate independence.

A Formula That Works

While I draw on a variety of research, experience, and parenting methods, I have found the formula prescribed by the gentle parenting method highly effective: acknowledge your child's feeling, address the action/behavior, and uphold the set boundaries/consequences. Gentle parenting is often confused with permissive parenting, and it's important to make the distinction between the two.

Permissive parenting is also different from the detached or neglectful parenting that we talked about in chapter 1. Permissive parents, like parents who gentle parent, are involved with their children, but permissive parents' involvement is often more about being their child's friend than their parent, and they often see any form of discipline as a hindrance to "letting a kid be a kid" or as a risk of their child getting mad at them or not confiding in them. When they do set consequences for bad behavior, they often don't follow through with them. Children of permissive parenting often have little respect for rules or authority, creating ongoing challenges for their child in environments that require adherence to rules.

Let's look at the same parent-child interaction through both lenses.

Your fifteen-year-old's school is only a mile from the house, but it's on your way to work, so you have agreed to drop your child off each day with one requirement: they must be in the car by 7:45 a.m., so that you can get to work on

Gentle parenting is often confused with permissive parenting, and it's important to make the distinction between the two.

time. If they aren't ready on time, they have to walk to school.

The first two weeks, they are walking out the door with you on time, and off you both go. The middle of the third week, you're heading to the door, and your child comes down the stairs talking away on her phone. She sees you at the door and gives you the one-minute sign as she heads to the kitchen. You take a deep breath, follow her to the kitchen, look her in the eye, and tell her it's 7:44 and you are leaving in one minute whether she is in the car or not.

Still talking on her phone, she gives you a glare and motions to the bagel she is waiting to pop up from the toaster. You walk out the door and get in the car. It's her first time being late, so you wait an extra minute. She doesn't come out.

Your daughter understands the expectations and the consequences if she *chooses* not to meet those expectations. What do you do?

Working with the permissive parenting method, you go back into the house and tell her that you need to leave. "Can't you just give me two minutes so I can get my stuff together?" she snaps as she packs the bagel in her backpack and then runs back upstairs to her bedroom.

You say again, "I'm leaving without you."

It's now 7:50 a.m., if you don't leave right now, you will be late for work.

"I'm coming!" she hollers.

And finally, at 7:55 a.m., you both pull out of the driveway, your daughter yelling at you for making her rush. "I told you that you need to be ready to go by 7:45 if you want a ride," you remind her.

"Well, we're going now. What's the big deal?" she asks as she turns the volume up on her earbuds.

Working with the gentle parenting method, you leave without her. When she calls you to ask why you could leave her behind and complains that she will now have to practically run to school to be on time, you empathize with her frustration and encourage her not to let it ruin her whole day. If her tone and words are inappropriate, you will calmly let her know that and tell her that if she is unable to speak to you respectfully, you will need to hang up.

Once you are both home at the end of the day, you will only address it if your daughter brings it up or if she is behaving rudely to you because she is still angry. In that case, you calmly empathize with her frustration again and reiterate the expectations and consequences.

At the core of gentle/attuned parenting is a parent's ability to regulate their own emotions—to remain calm and reasonable in the face of their child's overflowing emotions—and to provide natural consequences whenever possible. If a child is not on time for the bus, the bus leaves without them—that is a natural consequence of choices they made that resulted in them being late for the bus. The same holds true for the parent who is offering a ride if their child is not ready on time because of choices they made that resulted in being late. If someone speaks rudely or inappropriately to their teacher or their boss, it's not tolerated, and there are consequences for such behavior. Parents should hold their children to that same standard.

In which scenario do you think the daughter will be on time the next day? In which scenario do you think the daughter will better understand choices and consequences and respect others' time?

I'm not suggesting setting consequences and sticking to them is easy—it's not—but parenting requires us to commit to the long game of helping our children become responsible critical thinkers who grow into independent adults. The long game requires that we teach our children that they have choices and the potential results of those choices. As in this scenario, the gentle parenting consequence was natural rather than punitive. The daughter wasn't yelled at or grounded when she was late; she simply had to walk rather than ride to school. The mom provided guidance through expectations and consequences while giving her daughter the freedom to choose whether or not to meet those expectations.

Gentle parenting is centered on respecting your child's feelings and their stage of development. What would that look like for a younger child? Here are a couple of examples.

THE SANDBOX

Your four-year-old just came down the slide and caught sight of a big pail in the sandbox, just sitting there waiting to be filled. He runs over, and as he reaches for the pail, he knocks over a two-year-old who's squatting next to it, playing with another toy. The two-year-old has sand on her face and begins to whimper. Your four-year-old is happily scooping sand into the pail, oblivious to the two-year-old next to him. What do you do?

Working with the *permissive* parenting method, you do nothing. The two-year-old isn't hurt and she is being attended to by her dad, who glares at you but says nothing, and your son's happily playing and you don't want to disturb that.

Working with the *gentle* parenting method, you go over to the two-year-old and ask if they are OK: this is to be a role model and teach empathy. Now you take a quiet moment to talk in a calm voice to your son. "You knocked the little girl over and hurt her. That's not OK. How could you have gotten the pail and shovel differently?"

You validate any appropriate responses he provides and address any inappropriate responses. Now you acknowledge that it may be frustrating when someone is in the way but that it's not OK to knock someone over, and then offer appropriate options.

"You could have asked her to move. You could have come and got me, and I could have helped you. You could have decided to play with something else."

> Developmentally, the brain of a four-year-old does not understand these concepts unless someone teaches them.

You've established expectations for your son's behavior—he cannot push people aside—you've displayed empathy and concern for the child your son pushed, and you've helped him begin to understand that he has options when a problem arises. Developmentally, the brain of a four-year-old does not understand these concepts unless someone teaches them. This can sometimes be hard to remember when we see our child push someone over simply to get at a toy. We might react with anger: "What are you doing? You can't just push people over!" Because our adult brain understands that concept, we sometimes forget that, depending on the developmental stage of our child's brain, they may not.

Too often, children are punished for simply being a child, i.e., not having the neurological maturity to behave any other way.

—SARAH OCKWELL-SMITH, AUTHOR OF *THE GENTLE PARENTING BOOK* AND *THE GENTLE DISCIPLINE BOOK*

In this scenario, being the permissive parent and doing nothing when your son pushes over a child (and the other child is not hurt) certainly seems the easiest thing to do. But how easy will it be for your child when he's six, seven, eight and is pegged as the bully in school with no friends because he's still just pushing people over to get what he wants? It's not his fault he behaves this way if he has never been taught to behave differently, but he is the one who will suffer for it.

YOU'RE A ...

Your eleven-year-old is in a fit of rage because you don't have time to take her to the mall right now, and she screams, "You're a bitch ..." as she runs to her room. What do you do?

Working with the permissive parenting method, you do nothing; your daughter is just mad, and she'll get over it. Or you put what you're doing aside and offer to take her to the mall so she won't be mad at you.

Working with the gentle parenting method, you give your daughter a few minutes to calm down and then go talk to her.

"You sounded pretty angry with me."

"I'm the only one not at the mall right now. See?" she says, holding up her phone to show you the picture of all her friends eating and laughing at the food court.

"It's hard feeling left out," you empathize, "and I understand why you're angry, but it's not OK to scream at me and call me names."

"I know, Mom. I just really wanted to go. I'm sorry. They still want me to come. Can you bring me in a little bit?"

"Not today. Tomorrow, let's look at the calendar and see if there's an afternoon next week that I can take you."

You validated your daughter's feelings, let her know that screaming and swearing at you will *not* get her what she wants and that she can exert some control by planning ahead—all natural consequences appropriate for her developmental level.

It's important to note that if you have never parented your eleven-year-old this way and she is used to her disrespect being tolerated or getting what she wants when she wants it, the fairly easy resolution between mom and daughter above will not magically occur the first time you try it. You have committed to parenting differently, and you will need to allow your child the time to catch up. Late in the book we'll talk about strategies and coping skills as you guide yourself and your child into this new way of parenting.

In the real world, not showing up on time, pushing people out of your way, and swearing at people in anger have very real consequences. If parents don't teach their children that they have the freedom to make choices and that those choices lead to consequences, they will not be equipped to deal with life's very real consequences.

TAKE A MOMENT

When you think of the above three examples of permissive parenting and gentle parenting, assess which ones are closer to your parenting style. Or perhaps neither response is familiar to you, and instead you lean toward more dependency-, fear-, or reward-based parenting. In the case of dependency-based needs, the parent of the two-year-old would be sitting in the sandbox with him, directing every movement, and the parent of the eleven-year-old would have made sure they were able to get their child to the mall before they had an opportunity to be upset. None of us parent exactly the same way all the time; we all move along the spectrum below.

Take a moment to identify where on the balance you most often parent. Does it feel good to parent that way? Make a list of the reasons why or why not, and set it aside for now.

Gentle parenting is one tool that parents can use to find the balance between guidance and freedom that's right for their child.

BALANCE OF GUIDANCE AND FREEDOM

Permissive Parenting — Gentle Parenting — Hypervigilant Parenting

Other terms associated with gentle parenting are attuned parenting and conscious parenting. These methods of parenting share similar concepts to gentle parenting. A key concept is that the parent is able to emotionally regulate themselves and remain calm regardless of how distraught their child might be. Parents need to be the emotional container for the child in that moment, meaning they will accept and deal with the emotions that the child is having in that moment while remaining emotionally regulated themselves. It's the parent's role to stay attuned to their child's needs in that moment and not worry about their own.

A perfect example is a child throwing a temper tantrum in the middle of the store. The parent may feel the need to immediately stop the tantrum to avoid further embarrassment. However, addressing that need would not allow them to address their child's need to have their feelings acknowledged, be given space and guidance to emotionally regulate themselves, and then, when appropriate, have a calm discussion about better choices. It's critical that the parent follow through on the established consequences.

> Other terms associated with gentle parenting are attuned parenting and conscious parenting.

Again, it is important to recognize your child's age, developmental abilities, and temperament when determining appropriate guidance and boundaries and to make those boundaries known in a way that is clear to them.

Being attuned to your child's needs is continuous. It doesn't just occur when they are upset. It also means paying attention when they need more opportunities for increased responsibilities, and when they need more freedom and space from parental oversight.

Whose Need Are You Filling?

The playground is like a petri dish for researching parenting styles, and I spend a lot of time at the playground with my granddaughter.

Most of the parental hovering I observe in this setting appears to be about protecting the little ones from even the slightest risk of harm. But one day, I observed a mom and her son who must have been eight or nine years old. She was on his heels like he was a two-year-old. If he ran, she ran with him. If he climbed the stairs, she climbed up right behind him. If he slid down, she would come down and wait at the end of the slide to catch him.

It was obvious that her son was embarrassed with her constant engagement with him. He became irritated with her, asking her to stop. Instead of listening to what her son was asking for—space—her response was, "I don't know why you're irritated with me. I'm just trying to play with you."

The boy continued do everything he could to lose his mother, including doing flips from the bars, but she came along and did flips right behind him.

At one point, she said, "Let's play hide-and-seek."

He said, "I don't want to do that."

"Oh, come on," she said, "you know you enjoy doing that with me." And back and forth it went until he finally gave in and his mother went off to hide.

Through his actions and his words, the boy made his needs known—he didn't want to play with his mother. Mom refused to listen. She didn't attune to her son's needs. Instead, she filled her own needs. Whether her need was to bond with her son, or whether she was concerned that he didn't have other kids his age to play with and was worried he'd be lonely, I can't be sure. But she missed an opportunity to value her son's need for her to respect his space, allowing him to explore independently and possibly make new friends.

With Responsibility Comes Freedom

Our children are little human beings like you and me, and they can wake up on the wrong side of the bed, be tired and hungry and out of sorts, just like we adults can. All the same things that happen to us can happen to them. And we need to allow them to feel and experience those things. Instead of jumping in to make those feelings go away, we need to teach them the skills and provide them the freedom to learn to solve for themselves and to be responsible—the level of parental assistance needed is determined by your child's age, developmental abilities, and temperament.

Children will live up to our expectations of them. If a parent expects that their eight-year-old can't clear their own dishes from the table and fold and put away their clothes, then those things will be true. Conversely, if a parent sets the expectation (with appropriate guidance and encouragement) that their eight-year-old can clear their own dishes from the table and fold and put away their clothes, that, too, will be true.

Parents who support their children in meeting these responsible, age-appropriate expectations have children who get out of bed on time, get dressed, make their breakfast, get their lunches packed, and get out the door on time for school without their parent telling them what to do or doing it for them. No yelling, fighting, or rushing out the door.

There is freedom in responsibility. Freedom to choose which cereal you have for breakfast, what you're going to wear, whether you're going to make yourself a peanut butter sandwich or a ham sandwich for lunch. Confidence and a sense of accomplishment is built through responsibility. The eight-year-old who is confident in doing these things can help their five-year-old sibling learn to develop these skills—another boost in confidence! These are all building blocks in the development of capable, independent adults.

Dr. Richard Wadsworth, psychiatrist, author, and father of seven, speaks regularly to the importance of teaching children to be responsible for themselves. A video he posted sharing how his children independently get themselves up in the morning, make their own breakfast, get themselves ready for school, and get out the door on time without any parental direction garnered some angry responses.[8]

Some parents decried him as lazy because he should be doing all those things for his kids instead of making them do it. Others accused him of not letting his kids be kids. One parent suggested that kids had plenty of time to learn to be responsible when they grew up. Dr. Wadsworth responded:

"I taught them [my children] very carefully with love and encouragement how to use an alarm clock, get themselves up, ready, and on the bus on time. I don't remind them. They do it on their own, because I taught them with love and encouragement that this was their responsibility, and rather than rescuing them when they failed to fulfil a responsibility, I said, 'I'm really so sorry that happened to you. What can you do next time to not have that happen anymore?' It's actually a lot of work and very difficult to do this with my kids, but I've read a number of parenting books and psychology books, and I became convinced that this was the right way to go."

Wadsworth went on to explain that in addition to creating content for parenting advice, he also creates content for marriage advice, and the number one complaint he receives from those viewers is from women complaining that their husbands are lazy, irrespon-

---

8   Richard Wadsworth (@doctorwadsworth), TikTok, October
      25, 2022, https://www.tiktok.com/@doctorwadsworth/
      video/7158663073778404654?is_copy_url=1&is_from_webapp=v1.

sible, and don't pick up after themselves. Those husbands were once boys, who in all likelihood had parents who did everything for them. The expectation of irresponsibility that was set in their formative years has followed them into adulthood.

Teaching our children with love and encouragement to be able to take care of themselves is hard work, and it's a parent's primary responsibility. It requires energy, patience, consistency, and empathy. Doing everything for your children is easy in the short term, but it makes parenting much harder as your child gets older, and it's more challenging for your child to develop into a healthy, independent adult.

Reflections

- *Return to your list of why the way you parent feels good. Assess yourself honestly as to whether your whys and why nots are a result of your needs being filled or your child's needs being filled. For example, if permissive parenting feels good, is it because it fills your need to always be liked by your child rather than filling your child's need to learn responsibility, respect, and accountability? If, on the other hand, parenting with extreme control feels good, is it because it fills your need to always keep your child safe from harm or distress rather than filling your child's need to build self-confidence to explore the world around them?*

- *Now, take it a step further. If the way you parent is filling your needs rather than your child's, identify one daily activity in which you can commit to practicing attunement—recognizing and focusing on meeting your child's developmental needs.*

CHAPTER 5

The Freedom to Play and Grow

At every step, the child should be allowed to meet the real experience of life: the thorns should never be plucked from their roses.

—ELLEN KEY

W e don't allow our kids to play anymore. Yes, most of them are involved in some sort of play, sports, gaming, after-school programs, but it's all adult-controlled, structured play. It's rare to see children run freely through their neighborhood engaged in creative, cooperative, free-wheeling play. What was once the norm is now almost extinct. And that loss of free-wheeling, and yes, sometimes risky, play comes at a cost.

Free play allows children to test their own limits—how high they can climb, how fast they can run, how long they can hide. It also helps them test, understand, and adapt through cooperative play. They may anger if someone beats them, but they quickly learn that they need to overcome their anger or no one will want to play with them: they learn to regulate their emotions. They build confidence, and they begin to navigate the balance between risk and reward.

Today, the option for free play isn't even on parents' radar. Even at playgrounds—where kids are meant to run and play—parents hover over their children, telling them to be careful or to wait their turn, or lifting them to the top instead of letting them attempt to climb up themselves. Children are being told how to take every step, leaving them no opportunity to assess a situation and determine the risk and reward or the opportunity to stretch themselves and experience success: to believe that they can do it.

Loosening the Grip: Is It Worth the Risk?

Meet "Josh" and "Eve," a newly divorced couple with two young children. They had very different parenting styles, and they were seeking my help to better coparent their three-year-old son, "Sam," and six-year-old daughter, "Grace." Josh had grown up on a farm, riding a tractor and working with machinery from a young age. He was taught by his parents how to use the equipment and how to move around the animals, but there were still inherent risks.

> Today, the option for free play isn't even on parents' radar.

Once, he had caught his fingers in a piece of machinery. Although it was a frightening and painful experience, he did not suffer irreparable harm. His dad was there, but he didn't freak. He just took the necessary steps to safely free Josh's fingers. His dad reminded him why he had taught him to follow a specific process when operating the machine and made Josh explain why he hadn't done it that way. "I was trying to do a shortcut" was his reply.

"What did you learn about that?" his dad asked.

"Not to do shortcuts," Josh replied. As a result of his upbringing, Josh was good about encouraging and allowing Sam and Grace to explore and play freely.

Eve had been raised very differently. Her parents had been neglectful, which resulted in her living in constant fear. In her attempt to make sure she was not like her parents, Eve ended up parenting at the opposite extreme—focusing on her fear- and reward-based needs. Both parents were very loving and involved with their children, but how they engaged with their children were not the same. Those differences had a clear impact on Sam and Grace.

When the children came to my office with their father, they were curious and playful and giggly and enjoyed playing games with him. They sometimes tested the boundaries with their father, but he was consistent about setting limits and sticking to them. When the children came to my office with their mother, I saw two different children. Sam and Grace were hesitant, unsure of what they should or shouldn't do. They weren't relaxed and playful. The change in their behaviors was so drastically different depending on which parent they were with that their guardian ad litem (a guardian ad litem is a neutral person appointed by the courts to represent the child's best interest by investigating all available options and, based on those findings, make recommendations to the court) was concerned that they were being abused by the mom and that this was the reason they presented as withdrawn and anxious.

While that is sometimes a sign of abuse or neglect, that was not the case here. Eve was engaged and caring with Sam and Grace, but her own fears and anxiety were causing her to significantly limit their opportunity to play freely, take appropriate risks, be creative, and just have some unsupervised fun.

In her mind, Josh was neglectful and reckless, while she was responsible and attentive. She was making sure their children were safe by choosing their activities carefully and then guiding them in how to engage in those activities. This ubercontrol of everything her children did stemmed from her fear of them getting hurt and her appearing to be neglectful. It was an all-or-none proposition for Eve.

Eve chose to do individual work with me on her childhood trauma. Eventually, she came to understand that her trauma doesn't have to define her and that she is not her parents, and then we were able to work on her learning to relinquish some control for the well-being of Grace and Sam. Part of that process was to educate her on the importance of age-appropriate risk-taking and free play for children and then gradually exposing her to their risk-taking.

One activity was to let the kids bounce on the couch while she sat and watched without saying anything or interacting with them. I then instructed her to tell me how she was feeling. She would tell me that she was feeling anxious or sick to her stomach. We'd do some deep breathing together so she could calm herself, while the kids continued to bounce on the couch.

We engaged in these types of activities over a period of year, using bouncy balls or jumping on the minitrampoline in my office. "I'm afraid they're going to fall" was a common remark, as she, with tremendous effort, refrained from jumping up and stopping them. We talked about the risk that yes, they may fall, but there's nothing life threatening about the situation.

Gradually, Eve became more comfortable and came to enjoy watching her children play undirected without her anxiety level rising. We also worked on her playing with Sam and Grace and letting them guide the play versus her guiding the play. Over time, Sam and Grace became as comfortable being curious and having fun with their mom as they were with their dad.

Risky Play: It's Actually a Good Thing

In his article, *Risky Play: Why Children Love It and Need It*, Peter Gray, PhD and research professor at Boston College, makes the case for the evolutionary need for children to engage in risky play.

Gray outlines the six categories of risks, developed by psychologist Ellen Sandseter, that all children seem to be drawn to when engaged in play:

1. Great heights: Playing at great heights (e.g., climbing playground equipment, balancing on or hanging from a tree branch) helps children face fears and build confidence.

2. Rapid speeds: Moving fast (e.g., running, skateboarding, sledding) helps children understand and use their bodies.

3. Dangerous tools: Learning to use potentially dangerous tools (e.g., knives, ropes, power tools) helps children build useful and transferable skills and confidence.

4. Dangerous elements: Learning to navigate dangerous elements (e.g., fire, moving water, snow) offers children the opportunity to face their fears and understand the world.

5. Rough-and-tumble: Physical play with others (e.g., wrestling, chasing, sword fights with sticks) helps a child hone their physical and social skills.

6. Disappearing / getting lost: Playing and exploring in unfamiliar places (e.g., hide-and-seek, walking in the woods) provides a temporary scary thrill that builds skills and increases confidence when they overcome the scare.

Does thinking of your child engaged in any of these activities of risky play make your stomach lurch or heart stop? After all, we are tasked with keeping our children safe, so why, if we're in our right minds, would we let our children do any of these things? Because while we are tasked with keeping our children safe, we are also tasked with teaching them how to navigate safely *on their own* in the world.

> **TAKE A MOMENT**
>
> For each of the six categories above, list at least two activities that your child currently engages in and your level of involvement in that activity. For example, your three-year-old may climb the ladder of a small slide—are you holding onto them as they climb or waiting for them at the other end of the slide? Does your six-year-old know how to use a butter knife—with or without your assistance and supervision? Your nine-year-old is playing outdoors with friends—are you engaged in play with them or sitting in view of them, or are they unsupervised?

Our children, when they are still children and when they are adults, will engage in risky activities—we cannot prevent that—but we can teach them how to do it safely. If, at a young age, a child doesn't learn how to safely climb up the ladder of a slide or they're taught it's too dangerous or they aren't capable, how will they learn and develop the confidence to swing, jump, run, and play with other children? What else will they believe they aren't capable of? How will they develop the courage to realize their dream of becoming a firefighter?

If a child doesn't learn the proper use of knives and how to use them safely, when they do have the opportunity to use one unsupervised—and they will—they will be at a greater risk of hurting themselves.

According to Gray, "From the age of 6 on, I, and all the other boys I knew, carried a jackknife. We used it not just for whittling, but also for games that involved throwing knives (never at each other)."

Gray and his friends were taught how to be responsible with a knife in a way that was safe, engaged their creativity (whittling), and developed hand-eye coordination and control (throwing knives).

Gray fondly recalls the opportunities he had to engage in what Sandseter refers to as *dangerous elements* and *getting lost*:

"When I was 10 and 11, my friends and I took all-day skating and skiing hikes on the 5-mile-long lake that bordered our northern Minnesota village. We carried matches and occasionally stopped on islands to build fires and warm ourselves, as we pretended to be brave explorers."

Today, parents who allowed their children to engage in a similar, but much smaller, adventure would be labeled neglectful. And yet this type of free-range adventure builds independence, critical thinking, and experience, all crucial elements needed to become a self-sustaining, responsible adult. Gray and his friends were taught and developed these adventure skills over time. This is not to be confused with neglectful parenting, when parents have no idea where their children are, who they're with, or what they're doing. Guidance was provided, and the children were offered the freedom to grow from that guidance.

"In a recent survey of over a thousand parents in the UK, 43 percent believed that children under the age of 14 shouldn't be allowed outside unsupervised, and half of those believed they shouldn't be allowed such freedom until at least 16 years of age!"

"In a recent survey of over a thousand parents in the UK, 43 percent believed that children under the age of 14 shouldn't be allowed outside unsupervised, and half of those believed they shouldn't be allowed such freedom until at least 16 years of age!"[9]

Gray asserts that the dramatic shift that has occurred over the past several decades from the freedom to engage in risky play in the 1950s to the highly controlled, risk-averse activities of play that children engage in today has created another dramatic shift: the rise of mental disorders in children.

"The best evidence for this comes from the analyses of scores on standard clinical assessment questionnaires that have been given in unchanged form to normative groups of children and young adults over the decades. Such analyses reveal that five to eight times as many young people today suffer from clinically significant levels of anxiety and depression, by today's standards, than was true in the 1950s. Just as the decline in children's freedom to embrace risk has been continuous and gradual, so has the rise in children's psychopathology … children are designed by nature to teach themselves emotional resilience by playing in risky, emotion-inducing ways. In the long run, we endanger them far more by preventing such play than by allowing it. And we deprive them of fun."

This path to childhood mental disorders can find its root in the lack of play and opportunity to fail and succeed as early as infancy, when the child's first attachment bonds are being formed. Forming a secure attachment in which the infant feels safe and nurtured by their caregiver in a way that encourages them to explore, fail, and succeed is vital.

---

9   Peter Gray, "Risky Play: Why Children Love It and Need It to Protect Our Children We Must Allow Them to Play in Ways Deemed 'Risky,'" Freedom to Learn, PsychologyToday.com, April 7, 2014, https://www.psychologytoday.com/us/blog/freedom-learn/201404/risky-play-why-children-love-it-and-need-it.

In one study by Beatrice Beebe, mothers engaged in play with their child at different intervals between the ages of four months and eighteen months.[10] The results clearly displayed the significant impact of a mother's interaction with her child during play and a child's level of security, attachment, and self-confidence. In cases in which the mother allowed the child autonomy and offered encouragement in their play, the child was smiling and relaxed and independently reached for and played with toys. Those mothers would offer supportive statements like "Oh yes, I like where you're putting that" or "Where do you want to put that?" while staying attuned to their children's emotions and reactions.

On the other end of the spectrum, children displayed distress and overall feelings of giving up when their mother constantly tried to control their play. "No, that doesn't go there; it goes here" or "You can't do that; I'll do that." The mothers, unattuned to their child's growing distress (breaking eye contact, whimpering, shutting down) and need for security, continued to overpower their child and how they played. For these moms, filling their own needs to exert control eclipsed their child's need to be creative and supported. When children learn that everything they do is "wrong" and that they are not capable, they will surrender to the sense of helplessness that has been communicated to them. They will not develop the ability to solve for problems and will depend on direction from others.

There are college students asking for direction on how to get their clean, wet clothes out of the washing machine. In a video that I thought must be a spoof but wasn't, a college professor tells of students asking, "Do I actually need to put my hands into the washer to get my clothes out of there?" This is another scenario in which no parent

---

10   Beatrice Beebe and Frank Lachmann, *The Origins of Attachment* (Oxfordshire, UK: Routledge, 2013).

sets out to infantilize their child to the point of not knowing how to wash their own clothes by the time they are adults, but rather it is something that happens over time when we aren't attuned to our children's ultimate need to be self-sufficient and instead are neglecting our responsibility in helping them meet that need.

When we talk about the psychology behind play and free time, we're talking about the development of self-esteem, the understanding that "I can make mistakes and still succeed, that I can do it myself." It is in the disorganization of play and the disorganization of life where our learning is the most effective. Think about your own life, when you have had the biggest struggles and you made it through to the other side. Did you experience personal growth as a result? How'd that feel? When parents don't allow disorganization to happen because *they* are too uncomfortable with that, and they try to control every moment believing they can prevent their child from ever getting hurt, they inhibit their child's chance at healthy brain development.

Science tells us that the more we give our children the space to communicate, be curious, and experience new things, the stronger the neuropathways in their brain become.

Back to the Neurobiology of It All

The more you allow your children the freedom to explore their curiosity, share their thoughts and ideas, and experience new things, the stronger their neuropathway connections that build confidence, creativity, and critical thinking become. This freedom to explore must be gauged by the age of the child and their developmental level.

Bruce D. Perry, MD PhD, developed the theory of the neurosequential model of therapeutics, which indicates that our brain develops upward and outward *and* inside and out. In essence, we need to think of each layer of development as a piece of the foundation that builds upon itself. If an infant's basic needs aren't being met at that level of the basic brain stem—they don't feel safe, no one responds to their cries of distress, or, if they do, it's with anger and/or anxiety—that infant's brain will begin to have misfires of the neuropathway connections that must occur for the child to progress to the next developmental stage. The pathway that should be developing isn't developing, because the brain is being flooded with cortisol and adrenaline in response to the constant state of insecurity, of not knowing whether they are safe or not. Each developmental level of the brain must be as strong as the previous one.

When a three-month-old is screaming and crying, the parent nurtures and soothes them to help them calm down. A three-month-old doesn't have the ability to solve for themselves when they are hungry or need a diaper change. They are also not able to self-soothe every time they are distressed, so as parents, we must create the foundation of neuropathways that reassures them that they are going to be taking care of, they are going to be safe, and they don't have to be in fight, flight, or freeze mode all the time. By establishing those connections, they begin to understand that they are safe to reach out and explore their world.

At twelve months, a child is beginning to gain their balance, communicate through speech, and interact with their environment in new ways. At that child's age and developmental level, a parent will give a bit more freedom for their child to explore and experience. If they fall and hurt themselves, the parent shouldn't be hands-off and let their child deal with it on their own. They will need to go to their child, check in with them, and, if appropriate, encourage them to try again. What a parent doesn't want to do is make their child afraid of falling. If every time a toddler falls on their bottom the parent reacts in a panic, creating feelings of danger and uncertainty for the child, the toddler will learn to be cautious, to not explore, to not keep trying to balance and walk.

These misfires or lack of development of the brain's neuropathways affect the child's

- physical abilities: if a child doesn't continue to try to stand, balance, and walk as is appropriate at this stage, they will be delayed in developing those skills.

- social skills: exploring leads to more interactions with their environment and the people in it. A cautious, fearful child will not reach out and learn to engage in their environment, limiting their opportunity to develop communication and interpersonal skills.

- cognitive skills: a child's reasoning, critical-thinking, and problem-solving skills will be hindered by their ingrained sense of danger and may believe that fight, flight, or freeze are their only options.

Children whose building blocks of development aren't solidly formed often tend to have balance issues, learning disabilities, and emotional dysregulation challenges.

What Level of Risk Is Right for Your Child?

We know that every child and every situation is different, but we also know that there are appropriate levels of play for each level of a child's development. I've provided examples below that you will need to adapt to your child's individual abilities and needs. The key here is to honestly assess your child's abilities rather than deciding based on your own needs.

AGE-APPROPRIATE LEVEL OF PLAY AND INDEPENDENCE

3-year-old play

- Runs and jumps easily
- Walks upstairs unassisted
- Rides a tricycle
- Washes and dries hands
- Stacks 10 blocks
- Easily draws straight lines and copies a circle
- Can stand on tip-toes
- Uses spoon well and feeds self
- Dresses and undresses self except for buttons and laces
- Can concentrate on tasks for eight or nine minutes
- Independent play for up to an hour

4-year-old play

- Skip and hop on one foot
- Catch and throw a ball overhand
- Walk downstairs alone
- Draw a person with three separate body parts
- Build a block tower with 10 blocks
- Understand the difference between fantasy and reality
- Draw a circle and square
- Dress themselves
- Able to fasten large buttons without help
- Pull a zipper after it is fastened

5-year-old play

- Jump rope
- Walk backward
- Balance on one foot for at least 5 seconds
- Use scissors
- Begin learning how to tie shoes
- Draw a triangle and diamond
- Draw a person with six body parts
- Know address and phone number
- Write first name
- Start to help with chores around the house

6-7-year-old play

- Enjoy many activities and stay busy
- Like to paint and draw
- Practice skills in order to become better
- Jump rope
- Ride bikes
- Engage in free play. Kids can develop social skills and have more fun when left to their own devices. Playing tag, riding bikes, and other outdoor group activities not supervised by an adult
- Can do simple math like adding and subtracting
- Can tie shoelaces
- Like to play alone, but friends are becoming important

8-9-year-old play

- Like competition and games
- Start to mix friends and play with children of different gender
- Jump, skip, and chase
- Dress and groom self completely
- Use tools (i.e., hammer, screwdriver)
- Engage in free play. Kids can develop social skills and have more fun when left to their own devices. Playing tag, riding bikes, and other outdoor group activities not supervised by an adult

According to the age-appropriate level of play and independence for your child in the chart above, do they engage in those activities? If not, why?

- Are they physically incapable, and if so, what is their physical limitation, and can it be accommodated to help them get closer to that level of appropriate play and independence?

- Has your child never had the opportunity to develop that skill/independence? If so, why?

- What role have you played in limiting that development?

- Identify whether you may be holding your child back based on your own fear-based, dependency-based, or reward-based needs.

- How can you change the focus to your child's need and help them develop that skill/independence?

- If your child is engaging in activities far above their age level, assess whether they truly have the skills and maturity to do so safely or if you need to be more attuned to your child's developmental and age-appropriate needs and abilities.

Reflections

- *Review the activities you listed under the six categories of risky play, and compare them to the chart of age-appropriate risky play activities. Is your child participating in age-appropriate activities?*

- *If your child is not participating in age-appropriate play (they are either above or below their age level), look at the reasons why. If below their age level, is there a physical or developmental disability that is limiting their abilities, or are you holding them back based on your own fears and needs?*

CHAPTER 6

The Benefits of Freedom

Behind every young child who believes in
[themselves] is a parent who believed first.

—MATTHEW JACOBSON

We are wired to be free to think, create, trust, succeed, and yes, even fail. We are wired to be the best expression of ourselves. When children are allowed to grow up with freedoms appropriate for their age and developmental level, they reap a world of benefits. These children develop a sense of

1. security,
2. trust,
3. belonging,
4. curiosity,
5. responsibility, and
6. purpose.

All of which leads to independence, critical thinking, and experience. The benefits developed through a child's freedom to grow build upon each other.

So what does this all mean? As we've learned from Dr. Siegel and Dr. Payne Bryson in their book *The Whole-Brain Child*, and from Dr. Bruce D. Perry and his theory of neurosequential model of therapeutics, a child's brain develops upward and from the inside out, building one foundational block upon another. We've also learned that if a child's brain stem is locked in fight, flight, or freeze mode, they will be unable to form a secure attachment to their caregiver, and the next stages of development will be delayed or disengaged. It stands to reason that an infant who is secure in their caregiver's ability to love them and keep them safe will maintain a level of confidence that enables their brain to continue its development to the next stage.

When we feel secure, we begin to trust. When we trust those who care for us, we gain a sense of belonging to them. Our ability to feel secure, to trust, and to feel like we belong provides us confidence to be curious and explore our environment. Because we trust that if something goes wrong, our caregivers, our community, will be there to help us, we learn that we can make mistakes and still be loved and supported.

With more freedom comes more responsibility for ourselves (learning to put our own shoes on) and eventually for others (helping younger sibling put their shoes on). This increase in responsibility for ourselves and others leads to a greater sense of belonging—"I am a contributing member of my community"— and a sense of purpose. The cycle continues. An increase in a sense of belonging, of fulfilling responsibilities for the community (which can be family, school, team, etc. ...) lends itself to further development of trust and security in ourselves and those around us, which leads to more confident exploration of the world: building blocks that never stop.

All of this leads to a child's opportunity to make choices. This is where some parents really struggle. Providing our children the opportunity to make choices means we must relinquish some control. In doing so, our children will learn how to make informed decisions about themselves and how they interact in their world.

TAKE A MOMENT

Spend a day or two observing the opportunities your child has to make choices, and write them down. Put the list aside for now.

Let's look at some real choices children can make at different age and developmental levels. I want to stress that these are choices provided by you, the parent. This isn't about letting your child make every decision about what they wear or eat or where they go.

PRESCHOOL AGE

"Here are two outfits you can choose from to wear to school today." At this stage, the child's not ready to determine which clothes are appropriate for weather and level of activity.

"The vegetables tonight are peas and carrots. Either you can have both or you can have one or the other. Which would you like?" You put the vegetable(s) they choose on their plate. If they say they don't want any, resist the urge to get in a power struggle. Simply state, "Then you don't have to have any vegetable tonight," and move on.

ELEMENTARY AGE

"Do you want to ride to school with Mom today, or do you want to take the bus?" Be careful to only offer choices that you and your child can follow through on. If riding to work with Mom is going to cause everyone to rush, save that choice for a morning when everyone can easily be ready on time.

"Do you want to have cold lunch or hot lunch at school tomorrow?" If they choose cold lunch, that gives them time to figure out when to make their lunch (with appropriate guidance).

Be careful not to take away choices they've already made simply because it's not your preference. This begins to happen in earnest for some parents when their children are in elementary school and have homework assignments. If your child wants to color their leopard pink with green dots and you think that's wrong, do not take away the choice they've already made. Let them keep their leopard the way they see it.

> We parents might see how it can be a done better, but the goal isn't to complete this project at an adult's level; the goal is for the project to be done by your child at their developmental level.

Art and science projects are another area of danger. We parents might see how it can be a done better, but the goal isn't to complete this project at an adult's level; the goal is for the project to be done by your child at their developmental level.

MIDDLE SCHOOL

Bigger choices will be made as your child reaches the age or ten, eleven, twelve, thirteen. It's important to continue to be attuned to your child's needs, temperament, and developmental level, because the capabilities between children can vary greatly. While one ten-year-old may be highly confident and capable of staying home alone for a few hours, another ten-year-old may not have the capacity to be home alone for fifteen minutes. Know your child.

Your child has made plans (with your approval) to go to a friend's house after school. You offer them the following choice:

Parent: I can pick you up at eight o'clock, but then you're not going to have time to do your homework. Or I can pick you up at six o'clock, and that will give you a couple of hours to do your homework before getting to bed.

Child: I want to stay until eight.

Parent: And what will you do about your homework?

Child: I can do it with Johnny.

Parent: OK, so you are going to do your homework before I pick you up at eight?

Child: Yes.

You pick your child up and ask if they completed their homework. They tell you they forgot, but they'll just do it when they get home.

Parent: That's not an option. You said you would do your homework before I picked you up, but you didn't. You cannot stay up late doing your homework.

Child: But I need to get it done.

Parent: Doing it tonight is not an option. Can you think of any other options?

Your child might decide to get up early to get it done or go to school without it done. If they complain about not getting their homework done and that they are going to get in trouble, empathize with them. "I bet it will be hard for you when the teacher asks you to hand in your homework and you have to tell them you didn't do it. What do you think you could do differently next time?"

There is a lot of opportunity for growth in these simple scenarios in which you provide your child choices, consequences, and the freedom to learn from them.

HIGH SCHOOL

By high school, your child should have a strong voice in what interests them, what classes they take, what activities they participate in, what type of job they want, and yes, who their friends are. It's time to choose your battles very carefully, because there will be many, but that doesn't mean you forgo your standards and limitations. If your child is planning to go out in a shirt that says, "F everyone" and you believe that is inappropriate, you can tell them it's not allowed. Now, can they sneak it out and put the shirt on once they've left the house. Yes, you can't control that, but you can let your standards be known. If there is a consequence in the outside world for wearing that shirt, like detention or suspension, you can deal with that when the moment arrives.

A fourteen-year-old is only two years away from driving a car and four years away from adulthood. Four years! As parents, we might let ourselves pretend that adulthood is still far in the future, but the truth is it's right around the corner. How ready is your child?

FOOTBALL AT FOURTEEN

A mom I was working with came into one of our sessions very upset because her husband had let their fourteen-year-old daughter go to the school football game with friends.

"OK," I said.

"But Lisa, what about sex trafficking?" she asked.

"What about it?" I said.

"Emily could have been taken by someone and sold into a sex ring and we'd never find her."

From there we had a discussion about the realities of sex trafficking and that the number one way it occurs is not by random stranger abduction but through an older man gradually, over time, luring them into a relationship and becoming their "boyfriend," either online or in person.[11] We also talked about educating Emily on ways to be aware of potential danger.

The mom's anxiety level began to decrease. I asked if she had any other concerns.

"Well, she went with a group of friends."

"OK," I said, "What's your concern around that?"

"What if they get into trouble?"

"If they get into trouble," I said, "there will be a lesson in there for them to learn."

A fourteen-year-old will be an adult, free to make any and all decisions about their life, in less than four years. If the world feels too unsafe and Emily is too incompetent to navigate a school football game with friends at fourteen, she will not be equipped to be an independent adult at eighteen or twenty. She will still be out in the world as an adult; she just won't be equipped to make decisions that keep her safe.

THE CHANCE TO MAKE IMPORTANT CHOICES

Meet "Charlie," a fifteen-year-old young man I was working with who got into some trouble with his friends. They vandalized some houses and got caught. His parents let him know that they were disappointed in his choices, and they let him figure out how he was going to handle

---

11   Polaris Project, accessed April 11, 2023, https://polarisproject.org/human-trafficking/.

it. Charlie admitted his guilt and offered to pay for any damages. Because he stepped up, no charges were brought against him.

The real challenge became the fallout with friends who accused him of narking on them and didn't want to be friends with him anymore. We had some work to do to help him get on the other side of that, but in the end he realized that he didn't want friends like that. He also learned that he needed to pay better attention to who his friends were.

If his parents had chosen to dictate how he was going to deal with it and simply punished him—no discussion—his ability to critically think through that scenario and make the best decision for himself wouldn't have taken place. That critical-thinking experience prepared him for a situation he found himself in a year later.

Charlie, at sixteen, decided to drive with his friend to a party at what they thought was another high schooler's house. Once he got in, he realized it was a college frat party and decided he didn't want to be there. He tried to convince his friend to leave with him, but they wanted to stay, so Charlie left on his own. When I asked him how he felt about leaving his friend behind, he said he didn't like leaving them, but he also knew he couldn't stay, so he had to make a choice, and he made the choice that was right for him.

LOOSENING THE GRIP: THE FREEDOM TO NOT BE PERFECT

Meet "Yvette," who began counseling sessions with me when she was ten. Her parents were concerned about Yvette's high level of anxiety and told me, "I know we are doing something wrong; we just don't know what it is. We're supportive parents. We love her. We give her attention. We try do everything right."

Mom and Dad were high-achieving individuals. Mom was a dentist, and Dad was CEO of a large corporation. Dad had been raised in a neglectful environment and Mom in a hypercritical one. Both were extremely proud of their accomplishments. Because they had worked so hard to get where they were—a place that proved their worth—the identity of each parent was wrapped up in succeeding, and that identity impacted their parenting style. Their children needed to be good kids, they needed to perform at their best, and ten-year-old Yvette needed to be a positive role model for her three younger siblings. Being a positive role model was expected of her twenty-four hours a day.

Yvette was cracking under that intense pressure to be perfect. When she made a mistake, it couldn't simply be her mistake. It became a poor choice that reflected on the whole family. She was responsible for modeling positive choices for her siblings, not negative ones. Any time Yvette wasn't "perfect," she would have an emotional overload that would result in crying, screaming, slamming doors, and berating herself: "I'm stupid. I'm horrible. I'm the worst daughter."

Fortunately, the parents understood that this wasn't about "fixing" Yvette; it was about addressing the whole dynamic that brought her to this point. Both parents agreed that they needed to go into individual therapy to work on their own childhood issues and really deal with the pressure that they put on themselves to achieve and how to stop transferring that pressure to their children.

Yvette and I got to work on helping her reframe her beliefs and expectations about herself. That required her to understand that the pressure she was feeling wasn't pressure she was putting on herself; nor was it pressure to achieve what she wanted to achieve for herself. Instead, it was pressure from her parents to achieve what they wanted her to achieve. Here's where some freedom and choices came in. Yvette had to decide what she really wanted, what was important to *her*.

After giving it some thought, Yvette decided that it was important to her that she do well in school. It was also important to her that she be a good role model for her siblings, with one caveat.

"I don't want to feel like if I make one mistake I have failed my brothers and sisters miserably. That I have let the whole family down."

Now it was time to give Yvette a voice that would help reframe how she felt about herself and how the family functioned as a whole. When she was ready, we met with her parents. Using "I" statements, Yvette was able to let her parents know how she felt and what she needed.

"I feel hurt when I make a mistake and then it's compared to me ruining my siblings' lives. I need you to stop doing that." Yvette also needed to learn to use "I" statements to negate negative self-talk. When she found herself saying statements like "I'm stupid, I'm the worst" after making a mistake, she practiced first noticing when she made these statements, then taking some deep breaths and finally reframing the situation with more objectivity. "I only made a mistake. It's OK to make mistakes. I'm smart. I'm trying."

This was an eighteen-month process of Yvette growing more confident in recognizing her needs and giving voice to them in a respectful way. It was also a process for her parents to learn to listen and to validate Yvette's feelings and make efforts to meet her needs. While Yvette still has occasional panic attacks, her anxiety is better managed, and she and her parents continue to have open and honest conversations. When those conversations start to get heated, they all agree to walk away and come back together when everyone is calm again. Yvette is free to make mistakes, to be a kid, without feeling like her family's world will crumble as a result.

I saw Yvette a few years after she finished therapy, and while she admits they are still a work in progress, the now-confident young woman I saw was a testament to how far *they* had all come.

Reflections

- *Return to the list of choices your child made during your day or two of observation. If your child had little to no opportunity to make choices, take a serious look at what is preventing you from letting them do so. Identify at least two choices they could be making each day (e.g., which outfit to wear, whether to do their homework before or after dinner), and commit to letting them make that choice independently. Gradually, expand that list as appropriate.*

- *If your child is making too many decisions (e.g., dictating what's for dinner, if you go out or not, when you need to take them somewhere, whether they'll pick up their toys or not), it's time to look at why you've handed over parental decisions to your child.*

CHAPTER 7

Ready, Set,
Face Your Fears!

It's not only children who grow. Parents do too.

—JOYCE MAYNARD

After years of committing to be the best parent I could be for my child, of putting in the work on my own issues and learning to attune to my child and her needs, I messed up big time. It was my daughter's senior year in high school, and she was performing a song at her school's talent night. It was a huge song, "Wind Beneath My Wings"—a song I used to sing to her when she was a little girl. Leading up to the talent night, all I knew was that my daughter was singing, because she wouldn't reveal the song. When I looked at the program, the title had been blacked out—I would later learn that they had accidentally included the name of the song in the program and my daughter had gone through and blacked out all 550 programs so that I wouldn't see it and the surprise wouldn't be ruined.

Added to the mix of that night was my mother—a hypercritical person who has always made me feel bad about myself. My mother, my husband, and I were all watching the show, and finally it was my daughter's turn. She came on stage and delivered a beautiful speech about what a wonderful mother I was. She had them put the lights on me and asked me to stand up, and everyone clapped. I sat back down, the lights swung back to my daughter, and she began to sing … and falter. I immediately felt embarrassed and thought, Why didn't she practice more? Why is she making these mistakes? It didn't dawn on me that she wasn't faltering because she hadn't practiced enough; she was faltering because this was an incredibly emotional moment for her. She started over and sang it perfectly.

After the show had finished, my daughter walked up to me and smiled. I had tears in my eyes and said, "Thank you so much, but you probably should have practiced a little more." Her face just fell. To say it was a huge fumble on my part is an understatement. How did I let myself veer so far off course? How had I been so blinded by my own needs and fears that I had totally disregarded hers? I had let the pressure to meet my mother's unrealistic expectations take over. I had let her hypercritical comments about my daughter's dress, song choice, anything and everything seep into my own thought patterns. I had regressed in a big way, and I needed to repair my mistake.

I acknowledged to my daughter that what I had done to her was awful. I apologized and I asked for forgiveness, and over the next four years, I did everything I could to make it up to her. Then, on my forty-second birthday, we were celebrating at a karaoke bar, and my daughter stood up, looked me in the eye, and said, "You better friggin' cry this time." Up on the stage she went and belted out "Wind Beneath My Wings." Tears were streaming down my face; my daughter had finally forgiven me.

So are you ready to face your fears and commit to change?

Do I wish I hadn't screwed up? Absolutely. Do I regret all my hard work and efforts to be a good parent before this happened? Absolutely not. All those years of mostly getting it right is what enabled my daughter and me to repair my major mistake and me to learn from it. It's incredibly difficult to stay attuned and conscious and aware of what you're doing with your child at all times and to not overreact or shut down or just give up. But the effort is worth it, and as parents, we owe it to our children to be the best parent we can be for them.

So are you ready to face your fears and commit to change?

Facing Your Fears

Before you can make changes, you first need to identify what it is you need to change. If you are the type of parent who feels like they need to control everything in their child's life, you need to look at why that is. Maybe you parent from a place of fear that your child will be badly harmed or fear that others will think you are a bad parent. Maybe you need constant validation that your child likes and needs you. These aren't judgments; these are potential roots of how and why we parent. And if you don't know what these needs and fears are based in, you can't commit to changing them. So how do you go about figuring all this out? Here are a few of exercises to get you started.

THE INVISIBLE SUITCASE

We all carry an "invisible suitcase" filled with the beliefs we have about ourselves, the people who care for us, and the world in general. The beliefs and expectations we fill our invisible suitcase with are based on our life experiences, and for some of us, our invisible suitcase is often filled with overwhelming negative beliefs and expectations. A child who was neglected may believe that all caretakers are untrustworthy. A child raised by a parent who demands perfection may believe themselves to be worthless and incapable of doing anything right. These developed beliefs don't suddenly vanish when the child becomes an adult. Unless those beliefs and expectations are acknowledged and dealt with, we carry them with us wherever we go.

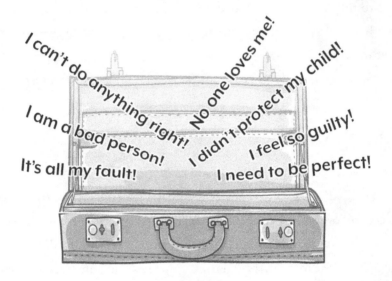

To find out what beliefs and expectations your invisible suitcase is filled with, grab a piece of paper and pen. Make three columns with the following headings:

- Beliefs and expectations about myself

- Beliefs and expectations about other people

- Beliefs and expectations about the world

This list is just for you, and it's important that you are completely honest with yourself about what beliefs and expectations you hold. Fill in each column. Does anything you've written surprise you? By seeing your beliefs and expectations staring you in the face, do you see a connection to them and how you interact/react with your child—both positive and negative? Think about the positive beliefs and expectations you listed. How can you strengthen those and use them to help overcome any of the negative beliefs you may have?

Are you holding negative beliefs and expectations about yourself, others, and the world that impede your ability to parent positively? Think about each negative belief you may have about yourself or others. Can you identify the origin of that negativity?

Practice reframing your negative thoughts into positive statements. When you think, "I can't do anything right," replace it with the statement "Today, I was able to _____." Fill in the blank space with one or more things you accomplished that day, no matter how small. By changing your mindset through reframing, over time you will begin to develop new pathways in your brain, until eventually, after consistent practice, it will become automatic.

Unpacking an invisible suitcase filled with negative beliefs and expectations often requires the help of a professional counselor, and seeking that help is a huge step toward the commitment to make the changes necessary for you and your child.

CATASTROPHIZING AND DECATASTROPHIZING

Catastrophize: To imagine the worst possible outcome of an action or event; to think about a situation or event as being a catastrophe or having a potentially catastrophic outcome.[12]

Who hasn't catastrophized a situation in their life? You make a mistake at work, and within seconds your thoughts jump to "I'm going to get fired!" You flunk an exam and immediately think, "I'll never graduate," which then snowballs to "If I don't graduate, I'll never get a job, make a living, have a place to live ..." We've all gone down

---

12   *Merriam-Webster*, s.v. "catastrophize (v.)," accessed March 22, 2023, https://www.merriam-webster.com/dictionary/catastrophize.

that rabbit hole from time to time, and that's normal. It becomes a problem when you're not able to step back, look at the situation objectively, and recognize that it is not a catastrophe and that you will get through the present situation. You decatastrophize it.

Decatastrophizing is a technique to reduce or challenge catastrophic thinking through cognitive restructuring.

Decatastrophizing is a term coined by Albert Ellis. It is a technique to reduce or challenge catastrophic thinking through cognitive restructuring.[13]

We can't control everything, but we can control how we think about things. It's all part of the rewiring of our neuropathways that we talked about in chapter 2. I help parents move from catastrophizing to decatastrophizing by walking them through their fears and imagining what would happen if those fears came true.

One mother whom I worked with, "Angela," was absolutely convinced that if she allowed her thirteen-year-old daughter to go out with a group of her co-ed friends that one or both boys would date-rape her. Angela was so convinced that she was unable to see any way to avoid it except to keep her daughter away from them. Her daughter was growing resentful of all the restrictions being placed on her, and Angela knew that overprotecting her daughter wasn't healthy, which is what lead her to me.

---

13 "Decatastrophizing," Psychology Tools, accessed March 22, 2023, https://www.psychologytools.com/resource/decatastrophizing/#:~:text=Decatastrophizing%20is%20a%20cognitive%20restructuring,home%20within%20a%20CBT%20model.

Together, we worked on decatastrophizing her fear. To do that, she first needed to walk through what would happen if her worst fear came true.

Me: "Your daughter went out with her friends and was raped by one of the boys. What happens now?"

Mom: "I guess I'd get my daughter help."

Me: "What do you mean by that? Tell me specifically what help you are going to get for your daughter."

Mom shared the steps she would take to help her daughter through this traumatic event. Then she went a step further and talked about how she would also get help for herself and would look at volunteering with sexual assault survivors. By walking step by step through the actions, she could take to get her daughter and her family through such a terrible event, Angela no longer felt helpless or that she and her daughter couldn't survive it.

The next step was talking through what proactive steps could be taken to further decrease the likelihood of this happening. Much of that consisted of educating her daughter on ways she could increase her awareness and control of her environment, like not allowing herself to be alone with a group of boys, listening to her gut and removing herself from a situation that doesn't feel right, not drinking from a cup that's been left unattended, and calling or texting her mom if she needs help, no questions asked.

It wasn't long before Angela let her daughter go to a co-ed pizza party and movie night at a friend's house. When she came to see me the following week, Angela had a smile on her face. "I did it. I let her go. I was scared to death the whole time, but I did it." To help herself reset during that stressful period, Angela did some of the deep-breathing exercises we had practiced. She also practiced reframing her mind, telling herself that her daughter was safe and that she knew what to do if she thought something unsafe was going to happen.

The best part for Angela was how happy and confident her daughter was when she returned home. I asked Angela, "Do you think you could let her do it again?"

"Yeah, I think I can," she said.

> ### TAKE A MOMENT
>
> Talking through what frightens us can help us normalize those thoughts and think through them more rationally. Here is a decatastrophizing exercise from TherapistAid. com that I encourage you to try. Start with one thing that you are significantly worried about. Write it down, and then answer the following questions.

1. On a scale of 1 to 10, how likely is it that your worry will come true? Write down examples of past experiences or other evidence that support your answer.

2. If your worry does come true, what would be the worst result that could happen?

3. If your worry does come true, what would be the most likely result to happen?

4. If your worry comes true, how likely is it that you will be OK in one week (_____%), in one month (_____%), and in one year (_____%)?

Decatastrophizing can't and isn't intended to eliminate all the feelings that result from a devastating experience. Its purpose is to help you figure out how you would work through it and realize that you would survive it.

CREATE YOUR OWN FUTURE

You've decided you want to make changes to the way you parent. What do those changes look like for you, and what will your future look like as a result of those changes? Draw or write out what that future looks like.

What things must happen to create that future? Do you need to be stronger on setting consequences, or do you need to let go of fears and be willing to let your child experience independence and growth? Do you need to give up the power struggle of "It's my way because I said so"? Remember, we are the creators of our own world. No matter what we believe, we make the choices about what we think and how we feel about it. Yes, there are things outside of our control, but even in those instances, we control how we react.

Committing to Change

You've identified areas you would like to change and what that looks like for you. Now, ask yourself these questions:

- Am I ready to make that change?

- Am I willing to commit to the hard work and effort required to make the change?

- Do I believe I can make the change?

Let's break those down a bit.

"Ready to make the change" isn't just about a willingness and a mindset; it's also the realities of your life. Are you going through a divorce or a job loss? Is your family in the midst of a relocation? If you are about to embark on a significant life change, you may not be emotionally able to add another big shift, and your children may not be able to either. If you and your family are going through a significant shift, your children are feeling it too. And when you do commit to working on making changes to your personal beliefs and expectations *and* how you parent, your children will also feel that. This isn't meant to steer you away from making the changes you need to make or provide an excuse not to make them. It's simply an opportunity to evaluate what level of commitment you can bring to the table right now.

Now, if you are ready, are you willing to commit to the hard work and effort required? This isn't a "I'll give it a try and see what happens" scenario. This is a significant and long-term change, and change is hard. Our brains want us to take the path of least resistance, to do what is familiar. It takes time and effort to rewire our brains in a new way. The process of changing how you parent isn't always going to feel good, especially early on. Your needs will not always be filled, and those things that made you anxious and fearful aren't suddenly going to go away. To push through them, you will need to get uncomfortable a lot. You will need to get comfortable with being uncomfortable.

Think of a change you've made in your life. It could be quitting smoking, saving money, flossing your teeth every day, or something simpler. Whatever it was, how did you make that change happen? Did you have moments when you wanted to give up? If you did, what got you through those moments, and what's keeping you on track today?

When I decided I no longer wanted to raise my daughter to be a brat, I had to wholly commit to a total overhaul of how I parented, no matter how hard it got. And it got hard. I had times of sadness, pain, frustration, and doubt—but I was committed to becoming the best parent I could be for my daughter. I didn't go this alone, and you don't have to either. Identify who the supports are in your family/friend circle. What other resources are available to you, like counseling, parenting classes, and wellness and parenting organizations like VeryWellFamily.com? Make these connections now, so that when you begin to falter, when you feel like you can't stick with it, you'll have people you can reach out to for support.

And finally, do you *believe* you can make the change? If you don't believe you can make the change, revisit your fears and your beliefs and expectations about yourself. What's keeping you from believing in yourself, and where is that doubt coming from?

If you know how and why you want to change, and you're committed to the long game, *and* you believe you can do it—get your supports in place, and make it happen!

Loosening the Grip: Changing How I Parent

Meet "Audrey," a single mom with two children ages ten and thirteen. Because of her own traumatic childhood, Audrey was fearful of many things, and that fear was dictating how she parented. When her children wanted to sign up for dance class or learn how to play tennis, her initial response, based in fear, would be no. Over time, her fears became instilled in her children. They, too, grew to be afraid of open spaces, of crowds; they were afraid at school, at the grocery

> Learned helplessness is when a person believes they are unable to control or change a situation even when options to do so are available to them.

store, wherever they went. The other result of Audrey's childhood trauma was a learned sense of helplessness. Learned helplessness is when a person believes they are unable to control or change a situation even when options to do so are available to them. It is a result of experiencing a stressful situation repeatedly, leading the person to believe they have no power over a situation and so they simply give up. The consequence of this belief would show up when she set expectations for her children.

"When I ask them to do something, like clean their rooms or put their toys away, they won't do it."

When I asked her what she did when that happened, she said, "I get frustrated, and I do it myself."

When her children didn't get themselves ready for the school bus on time, Audrey would drive them. The children would be late for school, and sometimes she would end up being an hour late for work. Those mornings were frequent and left Audrey in tears.

Audrey had a lot of work to do. First, she had to work through her own trauma history, which she did through individual counseling. As she made progress on managing her fears and overcoming her sense of helplessness, we also began working on her parenting techniques with a focus on allowing and encouraging her children to increase their independence and to set expectations and consequences with her children and stick to them.

Gradually, she began to let her kids participate in more activities, and with each new experience, they would gain self-confidence. Through her children's successful participation, Audrey also gained more confidence in their abilities and their safety, which in turn helped her allow them to have more independence and encourage them to continue to try new things.

Simultaneously, Audrey began to practice setting expectations and consequences for her children. The challenge, as it is with most parents, was sticking to those consequences. For children who haven't been held accountable, this can be a very trying time for them as well, and her children resisted. It took a year of Audrey really sticking to the boundaries she set before the children were finally on board. Through that year, there would be times that Audrey would come to my office, crying to me that it was too hard, that she couldn't keep doing this, that she was going to quit.

Every time, I would tell her, "You can be tired, you can get support, you can practice self-care, you can take a time-out for yourself, but quitting is not an option. You cannot quit." We would talk through a plan to get her over this hurdle, and that plan would help her through until the next time that it just felt too hard. Three years later, when asked if it was worth it, she unequivocally said, "Yes."

By the end of our time together, Audrey was able to let her sixteen-year-old go on a weeklong mission trip. Was she worried about her son going? Yes, but she didn't let her fear overcome what she knew was a great opportunity for her child. At thirteen and sixteen, her children are happy and confident individuals, who now get themselves ready for school and out the door on time every morning.

Get Ready to Reframe, Reset, and Repair

REFRAME

Audrey experienced success because she was willing to reframe how she thought about fear and her belief that she was helpless. Reframing refers to a change in mindset. For example, changing a mindset from "My daughter refuses to follow directions" to "My daughter is five years old and is still learning how to follow directives." Parents often think that their children are doing things just to make them mad, but that's rarely the case. Their child is simply using the skill set and understanding that they now have—based on their developmental level—to get what they want or think they need. Even though it may sometimes feel like it, they really didn't plot their morning meltdown just to ruin your day.

An exercise I offer parents to help them learn how to reframe is naming their fears as rational or irrational. "If I don't do x, y, and z, my child isn't going to be successful" is a common fear that drives parents to dictate their child's every choice and set unrealistic expectations for them to achieve. This is how I walk a parent through this on a rational-irrational scale.

Me: "What does being successful mean?"

Parent: "Well, I want him to do well in life."

Me: "What does that mean?"

And we continue to whittle down to what that expectation is. For some parents, their final response is "I want them to be perfect."

To which I ask, "Is that a rational or irrational expectation?"

Parent: "Irrational."

Me: "What would be a rational expectation?"

And we work to where the parent can acknowledge that encouraging their child to be the best they can be—at whatever level that is for their child—is the rational and healthy expectation for their child.

RESET

Audrey also took time to reset when she felt like she just couldn't stick with the changes she was trying to make. Resetting is taking break so you can reset your mood, boost your energy, or relax. Going for a walk, breathing exercises, meditating, and calling a friend are things people do to reset.

REPAIR

Repair enters the picture when we mess up, as I did with my daughter's performance. Repair is acknowledging to the person that you made a mistake, that you shouldn't have said/done what you did, and offering a sincere apology. A sincere apology is an apology with no "but you should have" at the end. When a parent takes this action, they show that they make mistakes, too, and that they want to do the work to repair their mistake because the relationship is important to them. It also demonstrates for the child that we can recover from our mistakes, that a mistake doesn't mean the end of a relationship.

PUTTING IT ALL INTO PRACTICE

An example I use in family and couples counseling of reframe, reset, repair is of dirty dishes being left in the sink (my pet peeve). My dad had a hoarding disorder, and there were always dirty dishes in the sink. They smelled gross, and I hated it. Early in our marriage, my husband was always leaving dirty dishes in the sink. Every day, on my way home from work, I'd brace myself for the frustration and anger I would feel about the dirty dishes that I just knew would be there. I'd yell at him that his leaving the dirty dishes meant he didn't love me. I attached all this meaning to it and would get really angry at him.

One day as I was driving home, preparing myself for the dishes to be in the sink, I thought, "Maybe he's not doing this to me on purpose. Maybe he's just forgetting he's putting them in the sink." When I got home that day, instead of getting mad, which he was always bracing himself for, I asked, "Do you forget you put the dishes in the sink?" I could see him relax. "Yes," he said, "I get home, I put them in there, and I have every intention of taking care of them, but then a phone call comes in or the dogs need to go out, and it just slips my mind, and then you get home and they're sitting there, and you get mad at me."

It was time for me to reframe my thinking from "He leaves the dirty dishes in the sink because he doesn't love me and wants to make me mad" to "He leaves the dirty dishes in the sink because he gets easily distracted and simply forgets." I realized that my frustration about the dishes was my own issue stemming from my childhood and had nothing to do with my husband.

Now when I get home and there are dishes in the sink, I say, "Hey, there's some dishes in the sink. Would you mind taking care of them?" and he does. I don't get angry. It still frustrates me, but now I can just ask him to take care of it and then take a deep breath and walk away to help myself reset.

THE COGNITIVE TRIANGLE

The **cognitive triangle** shows how thoughts, emotions, and behaviors affect one another. This means changing your thoughts will change how you *feel* and *behave*

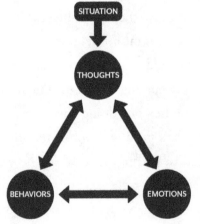

A **situation** is anything that happens in your life, which triggers the cognitive triangle.

Thoughts are your interpretations of a situation. For example, if a stranger looks at you with an angry expression, you could think: "Oh no, what did I do wrong?" or "Maybe they are having a bad day."

Behavoirs are your response to a situation. Behaviors include actions such as saying something or doing something (or, choosing not to do something).

Emotions are feelings, such as happy, sad, angry, or worried. Emotions can have physical components as well as mental, such as low energy when feeling sad, or a stomachache when nervous.

My final step in the process was to repair. I acknowledged that I had been misdirecting my anger toward him, and I apologized. By reframing my thought process, I changed my feelings about the situation and my behavior, which in turn improved the dynamic of our relationship.

We can do the same thing for our relationships with our children.

Prepare for a Struggle

We've talked about how your transformation and transition into being the best parent for your child will be challenging for you and will require work and adjustment. The people most affected by your transformation and transition—your children—will also find it challenging, and it will take time and consistency for them to adjust. Be patient with them, but don't confuse patience with allowing yourself to be inconsistent with them. Hold them accountable, but also give them grace when needed. Remember, they have

> Parenting is an evolution; no one magically knows how to do it all the moment their baby arrives.

learned to behave this way and will need your help to learn new, healthier ways to interact with you and their world.

Parenting is an evolution; no one magically knows how to do it all the moment their baby arrives. You will make mistakes along the way. We all do. Remember to give yourself grace in those moments, and instead of berating yourself for the mistake, learn from it, and build confidence. Equip yourself with positive support and resources that you can lean on, and gain wisdom from them along the way.

Reflections

- *Return to your decatastrophizing exercise earlier in this chapter.*

  □ *Repeat this exercise with other parenting worries you have.*

  □ *Review these worries three, six, and twelve months from now, and apply the same four questions. Have your worries increased or decreased?*

- *Identify a situation in which you want to reframe, reset, and repair. Make a plan for how to accomplish this and follow through.*

CHAPTER 8

Setting Up for Success: Prepare Your Child

The greatest gift a parent can give a child is self-confidence.

—STEWART STAFFORD

I f a child is used to their parent doing everything for them, and suddenly their parent flips the switch and decides the child must now be responsible for themselves, there is going to be significant pushback from that child. That pushback will be rooted in fear and uncertainty of the unknown. Preparing a child for new situations and transitions helps them feel safe and enables them to be successful. Just as you have prepared yourself to change how you parent, you must also prepare your child. How do you do that? Sit down and be honest about the changes you are going to make and why it's important. You will have to adjust the conversation for your child's age. For children ages three and younger, a full explanation of impending changes will not be needed, but you will need to acknowledge the change and be prepared to identify their feelings of frustration and explain that they can't always do what they want, and provide them other options.

Here is an example of potential conversation started with a high schooler:

I'm/We're going to try some new things. We realize that we have been putting too much pressure on you about school. You are getting older, and we need to let you start making more of your own decisions and have some autonomy. So we are going to let you start picking your own classes. We're also going to stop checking your schoolwork every day or reminding you about any homework or projects that are due. What we will do instead is check in with you once a month, just to see how you are doing with your grades and managing your workload.

Any child who has never had that type of autonomy will initially freak out at that level of freedom and responsibility, so it's important that you reassure them that you're not abandoning them. Let them know that you are simply recognizing the importance of allowing them to take more ownership of their own grades and the responsibility of that, and that you will still be there to support them, and that they can still come to you for advice or help if they need it. You just won't be directing them.

What about a seven-year-old who is used to their parent waking them up every morning for school, getting them dressed, tying their shoes, making them breakfast, and making sure their homework is done and in their school bag? Here is what that conversation might look like:

I'm/We're going to try some new things. Right now, I wake you up every morning, help you get dressed, make your breakfast, and pack your backpack for school. But I see you're not such a little girl anymore, and I know you are ready to do some of these things on your own. It will feel a little bit different for all of us until we get used to doing things in a new way. But I bet you will feel so good when you get yourself up and ready for school in the morning all by yourself!

It would be unfair to expect your child to make these changes overnight or even in a couple of weeks. It would also be unfair to expect them to make all these changes at the same time. Getting up and dressed on their own may be the two tasks you start with. Give your child an alarm clock, and teach them how to use it. You may still want/need to help them pick out their clothes, but make them responsible for getting themselves dressed. As they have success and build confidence in their ability to be more independent, add in making themselves breakfast and making sure their backpack is all set. If they bring a lunch, teach them how to prepare it the night before if possible.

Remember, you will need to *teach your child how to complete these tasks*. Do not expect them to suddenly know how to tie their shoes or prepare themselves a bowl of cereal if you have never shown them how. The same is true for older children. If you have always directed your child in exactly what they need to do for school and when and how to do it, you will need to *teach* them how they can do it on their own.

Once the child understands how to do the task that is being asked of them, set clear expectations and consequences, and make sure they understand them. Something as general as "You need to get yourself ready for school on time" may have different meanings for the parent than it does for the child. Clearly define what is included in your expectation of "getting ready for school on time." What exactly does that look like? What are the consequences if they do not meet expectations?

Consequences aren't meant to be punitive; they are meant to be an opportunity to learn how to become independent, which is not just about your child doing what they want but more about being responsible for themselves and responsible in their role as the member of a family, at school, and as a citizen. I am a huge proponent of natural consequences, but that isn't always possible. Whatever consequence is established, clearly identify what it is, make sure your child understands it, and then stick to it. Kids learn best with structure and repetition—make sure you can consistently follow through with the consequences you set in place and that they are appropriate for the situation and your child's developmental level.

As they increase their abilities and gain confidence, they will begin to feel better about themselves. Eventually, you will see the shift happen in which your child will initiate taking on more responsibilities, and it's important that you let them. It may be difficult for you to relinquish even more control, but if the new freedom or responsibility they are seeking is appropriate, you must attune to your child's needs and put your fears and/or need for control aside.

> # Eventually, you will see the shift happen in which your child will initiate taking on more responsibilities, and it's important that you let them.

Whatever process you decide is best for you and your child to make this transformation, you must make all expectations and consequences clear to your child. Depending on how drastic the changes are, it may take you and your child months, sometimes years, to make a full transformation, and even then, it will continue to be a work in progress. Your actions, guidance, and grace will be important to their success and must be appropriate for your child's developmental level, physical abilities, and emotional capacity.

TAKE A MOMENT

Take time to think about the changes you are about to make. Identify two areas in which you can commit to giving your child more responsibility. These areas should be stepping stones to the longer-term changes you will need to make to your parenting style. We will come back to these later.

Loosening the Grip: Shifting Dynamics

Meet parents "Dharma" and "Tyler," who have four children ages nine to sixteen. Through their work in couples counseling, they realized that their parenting styles were very different and that it was having a negative impact on their children. They had done the work to stabilize their own relationship, and they were now ready to make changes to how they parented. They laid out a plan for themselves, and then it was time to prepare their children for the changes.

"How do we talk to the kids about this, with so many different ages?" they asked.

I encouraged the two of them to first sit down and think about what tasks each child needs to be more responsible for and independent with, and how they were going to help them develop the skills to achieve that. Once that was complete, we walked through what the family conversation might look like.

"Jared, Sally, John, and Lily, we've decided that what we're doing isn't preparing you for adulthood and that we're not being the best parents we can be for you. So we're going to start working on helping you develop the skill sets you need for the age that you are. Jared and Sally, that means you're going to stop complaining that the younger kids don't have to do what you do. At sixteen and fourteen, we will have higher expectations for you, and you will have more responsibility than your younger brother and sister. Lily, at seven, isn't going to have the same responsibilities as you, but she isn't going to have the same level of freedom either. We want you to only focus on what you can and cannot do.

"Jared and Sally, you have both told us over and over again that it bothers you when we keep checking to see if you've done all your school work, and so we are going to let you show us that you can manage it on your own. We'll check in with you twice a month instead of every day, and if you feel like you need help, you can still come to us. The consequence of not doing your schoolwork will be poor grades and other restrictions the school may place on you as a result.

"John, we know you want to be able to play with the kids in the neighborhood without one of us always being there. We are going to start to let you have that freedom, and with that freedom comes the responsibility to let us know where you are and to return home at the time we say you need to be here. If you can't be responsible about those things, you'll lose the freedom of playing in the neighborhood.

"Lily, you are right. You are old enough to pick out your own clothes, and that freedom comes with the responsibility of taking care of your clothes. It is your responsibility to make sure any dirty clothes get to the laundry room by laundry day, or they won't get washed. It will also be your responsibility to fold and put away your clothes. If the clothes you want to wear aren't clean, you will have to figure that out.

"We're not going to punish you if you don't follow through on these responsibilities; you will have the natural consequences that result from your choices. That doesn't mean that if there are times that we think your actions need an additional consequence we won't do that, but we first want to give you the opportunity to learn from your mistakes. We are here to support and love you, and we will be here for you. Don't feel like we're just stepping out and leaving you to figure it all out on your own. You can come to us for advice; you can ask questions. If you need help, we'll assist you. We're just not going to do all these things *for* you anymore."

Dharma and Tyler had the conversation with their children. They said it didn't go quite as smoothly as it did during our role-play in my office, but they felt pretty good about it overall. After a couple of weeks, Dharma said she was doing well with John's new freedom but not with the others. The difficulty came back to worrying that she will look like a bad mom if Lily's clothes didn't always match or if Sally and Jared didn't do all their schoolwork on time. That was an opportunity to revisit her why, which was that she was neglected as a child and was overcompensating by making sure that no one would doubt that her kids were well cared for.

Two years later, it is still a work in progress, as is all parenting. There have been many family discussions since that initial one as they all navigate and grow through this process. But there is progress, and Dharma and Tyler continue to be committed to work to be the best parents they can be for their children.

Know Whether Your Child Is Ready

What would it mean to you for your child to be their most independent self? How do you assess whether they are ready for that next level of independence? And if they're not ready, what can you do to provide them the foundational knowledge and skill development necessary to be their most independent self? Here are common scenarios that many parents struggle with and ways to help you and your child move forward.

WHAT WOULD YOU DO?

1. Your four-year-old tells you they want to dress themselves for preschool, but it's something you usually do for them. What would you do? Here are some things you could do:

- Identify what knowledge and skills your four-year-old needs to do this activity successfully on their own. For example, they need to know how to

  - pick out their clothes (a four-year-old may not be able to determine appropriate clothing, e.g., appropriate for the weather, clean/dirty, preschool attire, but they can still be offered two outfits to choose from);

  - put on every piece of clothing independently;

  - button, zip, snap, or Velcro as needed; and

  - put on their shoes.

- Identify if your child possesses these skills/knowledge (not just that they can recite back what needs to be done but they've demonstrated that they understand). If they don't, now is a good time to teach them the skills they are capable of learning. If they do have some or all of these skills, it's time to …

- Identify the concerns that are holding you back from letting them dress themselves and how to address those concerns.

  - Is it faster and easier for you if you to do it? If so, how can you adjust the schedule or process to allow more time for them to get dressed on their own? Perhaps you could

* pick out their clothes the night before, and

* keep clothing simple—limit buttons and zippers.

▫ Are you concerned that they will get frustrated with the process?

* Let them practice when you have plenty of time to gently assist as needed. Remember, it's OK to let them struggle a bit as they attempt to figure out how to do things.

* If they do get frustrated, identify what is frustrating them and how you can help them address their frustration (maybe they are not ready for buttons and zippered pants or tying their shoes).

▫ Are you not ready for your "baby" to grow up? If so, you need to put your own need to be needed aside and help your child develop their independence.

2. Your eight-year-old wants to go to a friend's house to play. It is only two houses away, and you know and are comfortable with the family. You prefer to walk your child to the house and stay while they are there. Your child is upset and wants to go by themselves. What would you do? Here are some things you could do:

• Identify what knowledge and skills your eight-year-old needs to do this activity successfully on their own. They'll need to know how to

▫ locate the house they are going to,

▫ follow street/sidewalk safety,

- respond if approached by a stranger,

- understand that no one has a right to touch their body in a way that makes them uncomfortable,

- call home if they need help or feel uncomfortable,

- tell time and know when they will need to return home, and

- behave respectfully in the homes of others.

• Identify whether your child possesses these skills/knowledge (not that they're just able to recite back what needs to be done but has demonstrated that they understand). If they don't, now is a good time to teach them. If they do have them, it's time to …

• Identify the concerns that are holding you back from letting them go and how to address those concerns.

- Are you concerned that they will be hit by a car? What is the likelihood of that happening while walking two houses down? Are there sidewalks? If not, can your child cross the neighbors' lawns instead of walking in the street?

- Are you afraid a stranger will snatch your child? What is the likelihood of that happening in your neighborhood? Could you stand at your house and watch your child until they reach the neighbors instead of walking with them? Could they call to let you know when they are returning home so you can keep an eye out for them?

- Are you concerned your child won't behave at their friend's house? Are those concerns valid? Do they have trouble getting along with friends in other settings, like school, the playground, or birthday parties? If not, where do you think your concern is coming from? If they do have difficulty regularly getting along with others, you need to look at what might be driving those difficulties. Simply limiting their interaction with others will not solve that problem.

3. Your twelve-year-old wants to go to a movie with a group of friends, and another parent will drive them there and pick them up. You prefer to drive them yourself and be with them to make sure they are safe and that they have what they need—money, food, and supervision. They don't want you to drive them or be there. They want you to give them money and let them go alone. What would you do? Here are some things you could do:

- Identify what knowledge and skills your twelve-year-old needs to do this activity successfully on their own. They must know how to

  □ reach you if they need you or find help if they can't reach you,

  □ make responsible choices despite what their friends might encourage them to do,

  □ follow directions (e.g., "When the movie is over, wait for Craig's mother in front of the theater doors" or "Do not go home with anyone other than Craig's mother"), and

  □ be confident to trust their gut if something doesn't seem right or makes them feel uncomfortable.

- Identify whether your child possesses these skills/knowledge. If they don't, now is a good time to teach them. If they do have them, it's time to …

- Identify the concerns that are holding you back from letting them go and how to address those concerns.

  □ Are you concerned your child will be sexually assaulted or abducted into sex trafficking? While these are real concerns, it's important to make sure your level of concern is based on facts and not on headlines. How have you helped your child be age-appropriately aware of these possibilities and what they can do to limit their risks without making them afraid to go anywhere?

  □ Are you concerned your child will become sexually active if they hang out with friends unsupervised? Where is that concern coming from? Have you provided your child age-appropriate information regarding sex and their sexuality?

  □ Are you concerned your child will get into trouble? Where is that concern coming from? Does your child regularly break rules or exhibit behavior that suggests they would steal, destroy property, start a fight, etc.? If not, what is the root of your concern, and how can you manage that so that you can focus on attuning to your child's needs?

4. Your sixteen-year-old wants to get their driver's license, like all their friends. You are worried that they could get in an accident and don't want them to get their license until they are seventeen. What would you do? Here are some things you could do:

- Identify what knowledge and skills your sixteen-year-old needs to have to do this activity successfully on their own. They must know how to

- ▫ pass state-required driver's exams,

- ▫ follow the rules of the road,

- ▫ react quickly and appropriately in a potentially dangerous situation,

- ▫ keep their cool and stay focused in a stressful situation,

- ▫ make responsible choices, even when under pressure from peers, and

- ▫ understand the dangers of cell phone use and other distractions while driving.

- Identify whether your child has the opportunity to develop this skills/knowledge through available resources like driver education, time spent practicing, driving with a parent, etc. If those opportunities are available for your child to participate in but you won't let them, it's time to …

- Identify the concerns that are holding you back from letting them get their license at an age-appropriate time, and address them.

  - ▫ If you're concerned that they will not be able to learn to follow the rules of the road or won't be able to pay attention while driving, going through the process of driver's education and driving tests for their license will help clarify that concern.

  - ▫ If you're concerned that they are "too immature," clarify what that means, and identify specific behaviors in which your child demonstrated that level of immaturity. Be honest as to whether you are using the label of immature as an excuse to keep them dependent or to address your own fears.

Every child is unique. There are guidelines for what's appropriate for certain ages, but there is no one-size-fits-all for any age. One three-year-old may need to be told only once not to wander into the road while playing in the yard, and in the yard they will stay. Another three-year-old may be easily distracted and need constant direction to remain in the yard and away from the road. I have known identical twins who had very different temperaments and skill development. At the age of ten, one of them could play out with the neighborhood children for a couple of hours unsupervised and be fine, while the other one felt better returning home every fifteen minutes or so to check in with his mother and let her know what they were doing. Educate yourself on your child's development, and offer them the guidance to reach the level of responsibility and autonomy that they are ready for.

You've got this. Now go parent.

> Every child is unique. There are guidelines for what's appropriate for certain ages, but there is no one-size-fits-all for any age.

Reflections

- *Return to the two stepping stones you are prepared to commit to today that will give your child more responsibility. After reading the examples in the section "Know Whether Your Child Is Ready," are your stepping stones still appropriate, or is your child ready to do more?*

- *Once you determine your next steps, make a plan for how you will implement those changes.*

- *Write down the conversation you will have with your child to prepare them for these changes. Practice the conversation with your partner or friend or in front of the mirror until you are confident in your commitment to sticking to these changes.*

CHAPTER 9

Go Parent

Respond to your children with love in their worst moments, their broken moments, their angry moments, their selfish moments ... because it is in their most unlovable human moments that they most need to feel loved.

—L. R. KNOST

There is a balancing act that parents must do: be the firm, guiding teacher who can uphold rules and consequences, and who is also fair, kind, and calm, a guide who offers structure and consistency while allowing their child the autonomy to make mistakes, take risks, learn new things, and play freely within that structure so that they may develop the skills and abilities to grow into a responsible, capable adult. It's all about finding the balance, attuning to your child's needs, regulating (both your child's and your) emotions, and allowing your child to experience consequences.

Loosening the Grip: You Are Not Your Child's Friend

Meet "Tonya," a single mom of a fifteen-year-old "Gayle." Tonya was only twenty when she had Gayle and had always prided herself on being more of a friend than parent to her daughter. When Gayle reached her teen years, she grew embarrassed by her mom's constant need to hang out with her and her friends. When they first came to meet with me, Tonya shared that she was the "cool" mom. "All the kids want to go to the mall with me because I'm such a cool mom. They tell me all the gossip." Tonya went on to explain how important it was to her that she and her daughter have a very close relationship, that Tonya and her mother did not have one because her mother was so strict, and that she wanted to make sure she wasn't that strict so her children would know that they were always loved.

> It's all about finding the balance, attuning to your child's needs, regulating (both your child's and your) emotions, and allowing your child to experience consequences.

Gayle was sitting next to her mother, rolling her eyes. Tonya was unaware. Once Tonya had finished, I asked to speak alone with Gayle, who told me, "She acts like she's fifteen. She talks to my friends, trying to use our slang. It's embarrassing. My friends think it's kind of gross that she's always hanging out with us. I hate it."

Tonya was not the cool mom. She was the unattuned mom who had no idea how her parenting, or lack thereof, was negatively affecting her daughter. Tonya was focused on filling her own need to not be like her own mother and to always be liked by her daughter. Gayle, while she liked her mother's "no rules" philosophy, allowing her to stay out as late as she wanted and letting her boyfriend stay over (what teenager wouldn't?), still recognized this was not normal.

Tonya's sister had a daughter Gayle's age, and Gayle respected the type of parent her aunt was. "My aunt is fun, but she's appropriately fun. She won't let my cousin stay out past midnight, which sometimes frustrates me because I want to hang out with her, but I think that's a good thing—to have some rules. My aunt would never let my cousin drink, but my mom lets me have wine with her all the time."

With Gayle's permission, I spoke to her mother alone and shared her feelings. It was a tough conversation, letting a mom who thinks she's doing a wonderful job know that she's getting some significant things wrong. Tonya was understandably emotional and said that all she wanted was a close relationship with her daughter. I let her know that giving Gayle total freedom, basically not parenting her, was not the way to achieve that. As parents, it's our role to provide structure and offer guidance, support, and love. That requires us to establish expectations and boundaries and to sometimes say no.

Over the next six months, Tonya and I worked on parenting methods and separating herself from her own mom. Eventually, she was able to acknowledge that setting boundaries and establishing appropriate expectations and consequences is not the same as hitting Gayle with belt or grounding her for a month for the smallest infraction, the way her mother did. Gayle was atypical in that she didn't complain about the new rules and structure her mother was establishing; in fact, she welcomed them, and their relationship was stronger for it.

Accepting that your child will get angry with you and even, at times, not like you can be a challenge for parents. Many parents do what they can to avoid making their child angry with them or, if they do get angry with them, make inappropriate concessions to get their child to stop being angry with them. While in the moment it may provide relief for the parent to "be liked" by their child again, it does not benefit the child, and the only person's need it is filling is the parent's need to feel loved.

For parents who are struggling with this, I often ask them, "Have you ever gotten angry at your significant other?" And every one of them laughs and says, "Of course I have." Then I ask if they stopped loving their significant other when they were angry with them. Many of them will confess that they didn't like them in the moment, but no, they did not stop loving them just because they made them mad. The same is often true with our own parents or our friends: when we get angry with the people we love, we don't stop loving them. Your child may test your patience at times, but you still love them, right? They still love you, too, even when they're screaming, "I hate you!"

Humans are capable of holding multiple emotions at once. It is not an either/or proposition. "Either you make me happy and I love you, or you make me mad and I hate you" is not reality. Show your child that you are confident in their love even when they are upset with you, and they will feel confident that you love them even when you are upset with them. Emotions can be messy and intense, especially when they are connected to those we love, and we need to learn how to regulate our own emotions and help our children learn to regulate theirs.

Regulate Your Emotions

In chapter 4, I talked about the need for parents to be their children's emotional container: to just be with their child and their feelings, and let them know they will love them and keep them safe no matter how intense those feelings may be. To do that effectively, parents must have the ability to regulate their own emotions. If their child is screaming and yelling in anger, the least effective thing a parent could do is scream and yell back. They may want to, but it will only serve to escalate the situation and devalue their child's feelings. Keeping our cool in tough parenting situations is not an easy task, and it is one that requires an understanding of how to regulate our emotions and then practicing techniques to help us do it instinctually. So where do our emotions originate, and how can we best navigate them?

The vagus nerve is the longest cranial nerve in the body, connecting the brain stem to our internal organs, and plays a key role in helping us regulate our emotions. It is part of the autonomic nervous system, comprising the sympathetic and the parasympathetic systems. The sympathetic nervous system is a network of nerves that gets us ready for our fight-or-flight response when the body is preparing for action. I think of it as our gas pedal: it revs us up and gets us ready to go. The parasympathetic nervous system is designed to restore the body to a calm and balanced state. It is like the brake that helps us slow down and reach a resting state. Sometimes our brake is broken, and we end up running on our sympathetic system all the time, meaning our gas pedal is pushed down and we're always ready for action, ready for fight or flight.

What happens when our body triggers the fight-or-flight response? The back part of our brain activates and hijacks the front part of our brain, where all our reasoning and critical thinking takes place. If you are in that mode, and your kids start fighting, yelling, and screaming, your brain is not able to think clearly, and instinctively, you will begin to yell and scream back. Now, when we step back and look at the situation in a calm state, we know that engaging in that way is not productive, but in the heat of the moment, when our sympathetic system is fully engaged, our fight-or-flight response kicks in.

The good news is that when this happens, there are things we can do to "reset" our vagus nerve. Deep breathing is one of the most effective ways of resetting our vagus nerve, because this is the nerve that controls our breathing and helps lower our heart rate. Even better, we can practice deep-breathing exercises in our daily lives so that they become instinctual behaviors as soon as our body feels like it's revving up. But before we talk about specific deep-breathing practices, let's talk about how to manage emotionally tense situations when deep breathing just isn't going to work in that moment.

WALK AWAY

If your child is having a meltdown—yelling, screaming, throwing things—and you're unable to calm yourself down *and* your child is safe, walk away. Don't storm out of the room. Look at your child and as calmly as you can say, "I'm angry right now. I can't talk to you right now, so I'm going to step out for a little bit. I'm going to go calm down, and I will be back in a few minutes." Depending on the age of your child and the situation, you can set guidelines for them while you're calming down: "You can sit and color or you can go watch TV, but you can't leave the house."

When someone's anger is increasing, it's critical that you give them physical space (this may include not looking at them), remain calm and quiet, and give them time to regroup if they are able. If your child's behavior is putting them or others at risk of harm and you cannot physically contain your child, you need to remain calm and quiet, call the police, and observe at a safe distance.

JUST BREATHE

Slowing our heart rate is a first step in engaging our "brake," or our parasympathetic nervous system, and we have the power to intentionally do that by controlling our breath. Like changing your parenting style, learning these techniques takes time, patience, and practice. When I first made my parenting shift and began working on regulating my anger, I would frequently need to step out of the room to calm down. There were times that I was so pumped on adrenaline that I would need to pace for a bit before I could calm my body enough to allow me to focus on deep breathing. It took time and a lot of self-discipline for me to practice deep-breathing exercises and learn to consciously engage in it when I could feel my frustration or anger bubbling up. Now, many years later, I find myself breathing deeply before I cognitively realize that my stress level is rising—my body recognizes the need before I do.

TAKE A MOMENT

Before we can begin to regulate our emotions, we must first recognize when we are acting upon our emotions. Over the next twenty-four hours, pay attention to whe you begin to feel angry, anxious, stressed, or fearful. Use the emotions thermometer below to make a list of those feelings and what is happening around you when those feelings surface. Set the list aside for now.

DEEP-BREATHING EXERCISES

There are a variety of deep-breathing techniques, and it's important that you find the ones that work best for you. Here are just a few exercises to get you familiar with how deep breathing works. I encourage you to try them and others but caution you against giving up too soon if it doesn't feel like it's working. It may not work the first few times—or ten times—and even when it does work, it may not offer you immediate relief. Depending on the circumstance and how comfortable you have become with the exercises, it may take several minutes for your parasympathetic system to return your body to a restful state. Time, patience, and practice is key: I promise it will be worth it.

Four Square

This exercise requires you to breathe in through your nose for a count of four, hold your breath for a count of four, and then breathe out through your mouth for a count of four. The breath out is like letting air out of a balloon and requires your

FEELINGS THERMOMETER

10 I am exploding out of control
9 I am ready to explode
8 I am boiling
7 I am heating up
6 I am getting uncomfortable
5 This is hard but I am in control
4 I am okay
3 I am cool and collected
2 I am relaxed and happy
1 I am feeling great!

diaphragm to be relaxed. To do that, your breaths in and out are from your abdomen rather than your lungs/chest. If you place your hand in the center of your abdomen and can feel its rise and fall with each breath in and out, you know you are doing it correctly. Keep breathing in for four, holding for four, and exhaling for four until you feel your heart rate go down. Continue for several minutes until you feel calm and at rest.

3-9-6

For this exercise, breathe in through the nose to the count of three, hold your breath for the count of nine, and then breathe out slowly and evenly through your mouth to the count of six. Like Four Square, your breaths in and out fill and deflate your abdomen rather than your chest. Repeat the pace and sequence of breaths for several minutes until you feel calm and at rest.

Hand Breathing

If you are a person who does best with a visual aid, give hand breathing a try. This is a good one to practice with your child. Spread the fingers of one hand. With the other hand, begin to trace your finger up the outside of your thumb. Take a slow breath in through your nose as you do this. Once you reach the top of your thumb, begin to breathe slowly out your mouth while tracing down the inside of your thumb. Breathe in again and trace up the side of your pointer finger and trace down the other side of your pointer finger as you breathe out. Continue until you have traced all your fingers. Repeat as needed until you feel calm and at rest.

CROSSING THE MIDLINE

We know that when we are anxious, stressed, or angry, our sympathetic nervous system kicks into high gear and blocks us from accessing our cognitive functions. One way to remove that block is by crossing our midline. The midline is an imaginary head-to-feet line down the center of your body. When you cross parts of your body from one side to the other, like crossing your legs or giving yourself a hug, the corpus collosum—the nerve system that connects both sides of the brain—is activated. When both sides of our brain are activated, we can think with our whole brain, and in doing so, we create a calmer, more focused mind.

This can be especially useful when we begin to feel anxiety creeping in, but we aren't in a situation where we can do our deep breathing, like when we are engaged in conversation. In this case, simply crossing one hand over the other will get us crossing our midline. This is a simple and useful tool for children as well. For a more energized crossing of the midline, toe touching, touching left toes with right hand and vice versa, works great!

Whether it's deep breathing, crossing the midline, calling a friend, going for a walk, or another reset technique, what is critical is finding the ones that work for you and putting them into practice, because it is essential that we, as parents, regulate our emotions. In doing so, we can care for our children in a healthy, caring way and be an emotionally regulated role model for them.

NAME IT TO TAME IT

When we talk about regulating our emotions and being an emotional container for our children, it doesn't mean we dismiss our emotions; it means we don't let our emotions control our actions. That is an important distinction. As Dr. Siegel says, "You have to name it to tame it," and that requires us to acknowledge and honor our feelings. It's normal and OK to feel overwhelmed, angry, or hurt when you're running late and your four-year-old refuses to get in his car seat or when your teenager angrily yells at you one minute and five minutes later is asking you to give them a ride to the mall. It's what you do with those feelings both during and after the storm that matters. Ignoring our feelings or pretending that we aren't feeling them is harmful to ourselves and those we interact with.

Feeling is the path to healing. There is no other way.

Emotions are chemicals, and they will leak if not addressed. Have you ever been in the checkout line and, once you reach the cashier, you smile and say hello, and they respond with a scowl and a grunt? They have never met you until this moment, so how could they be angry with you? They're not. Something else has made them

> # Feeling is the path to healing. There is no other way.

angry, sad, or frustrated, and they brought that emotion with them to work, and they are leaking it all over their customers. A coworker who has had a fight with their partner before heading into the office may dash by your desk with their head down and barely a wave. They aren't trying to be rude or avoid you. They just haven't figured out what to do with their feelings about the fight, and they are leaking those emotions with every step they take.

Our children's outbursts are often emotions that are leaking all over the place because they just don't know what to do with them. And sometimes we let our emotions leak on our children if we're not paying attention. We all have tough days and bad moods, but it's important to not let our negative emotions go ignored or spill over onto the innocent bystanders in our life.

Sometimes, we just don't give ourselves enough time to simply feel our feelings or take time to process them, but then once we do make the time to do that, we are fine. When feelings are continually suppressed or ignored over an extended period, physical and mental health issues can develop. Depression, substance abuse, and hypervigilance are potential consequences that stem from suppressed feelings.

Make time to check in with yourself. If you're feeling anxious, acknowledge that feeling and then ask yourself why. If you're feeling sad or angry, acknowledge it and then ask yourself why. Identify the feeling, accept the feeling, and then you can take steps to work through it. Remember, "you have to name it to tame it."

Set Clear Consequences, and Stick to Them

Consequences of our behavior are a fact of life. If you continually arrive late for work, disciplinary actions will likely follow. If you are caught speeding, you will incur a fine. Consequences are not all negative. If you work hard and are a responsible employee, you will likely be rewarded. If you maintain a clean driving record, you will save money on your insurance. We all learn from our own behavior by experiencing the consequences (good or bad) of that behavior, and when the consequence is natural, the lesson is more impactful and the learning curve quicker.

If a child pays attention in school, does their homework, and studies for exams, chances are good they will do well on tests and receive a good grade. If a child does not pay attention, does not do their homework, and does not study for tests, well, you can see where this is going. Both are natural consequences that provide them the opportunity to figure things out for themselves (depending on the age) and gain confidence in doing so. No lecturing (which doesn't work anyway) involved. If your child continually does not do well in school, additional consequences may be needed but *only* after the root cause of their lack of attention or completion of work is identified. Is a learning disability involved? A difficult school situation with a friend or teacher? Are you setting the necessary expectations and consequences at home to put them on the path to success in school? Each of these scenarios may require a different set of expectations and consequences—and sometimes a change in the parent's behavior.

When children are not provided the opportunity to learn from the results of their own actions or are taught inappropriate consequences to their behavior, the longer they continue on that path, the more difficult it will be for them to navigate life.

Loosening the Grip: Inappropriate Rewards Lead to Inappropriate Behaviors

Meet "Julie" and her eight-year-old daughter "Celia." Julie sought counseling for her daughter because when Celia wasn't given a toy that she wanted, she would throw herself down on the ground, kicking and screaming or holding her breath until she got it. Why was this eight-year-old still having tantrums like a two-year-old? Because her mother taught her to expect a new toy every time they went into a store, and by the time Celia was eight and Julie decided it wasn't such a good idea after all, Celia wasn't on board with the change.

These types of inappropriate rewards can happen innocently enough. For Julie, it started when Celia was two. "She always behaved so well, and I wanted to let her know that I was proud of her." Fast-forward to six years of Celia being inappropriately rewarded for what should be expected behaviors, and Julie was pushed to get help to fix the problem.

One of my first questions to Julie was "What's your plan to rectify the situation?" Julie looked at me, puzzled. "This isn't Celia's fault. You created this," I told her.

"I was hoping you could help Celia stop throwing tantrums," Julie said.

"I can certainly teach her how to regulate her emotions, but only you can undo what you have created."

Fortunately for Julie, her mother

> # Inappropriate rewards can happen innocently enough.

was someone she could lean on for support throughout this process. In fact, it was her mom's refusal to take Celia anywhere anymore that was the final push to get Julie to deal with the problem. Her mom joined the counseling sessions I had with Julie, and I learned that she had warned Julie when Celia was three to stop constantly rewarding her with a new toy. When I asked how she knew it would become a problem, she said, "Because I did it with Julie." When asked why she had begun this practice, she said that she wanted Julie to be happy, to feel special, and to know that she loved her.

This was good for Julie to hear. "I don't remember getting everything I wanted," she said to her mother.

"That's because I put an end to it early on when I saw that it was becoming a problem, and I realized that I didn't need to give you things in order to let you know that I loved you," said her mother. Here again, what was intended to be well meaning snowballed into an inappropriate consequence that created unnecessary challenges for both the parent and the child.

Over time, Julie's commitment and patience to not give in to Celia's tantrums and Celia's understanding and practice of how to help herself regulate her emotions turned things around for both of them. It's rarely a parent's goal to teach their children to behave badly. The key to good parenting is to look beyond the behavior and identify the cause. While there are a variety of reasons why a child may act out, how a child is parented—no matter how lovingly—is often at the root of inappropriate behavior.

APPLYING NATURAL CONSEQUENCES

Natural consequences can be challenging for a parent. You see your child struggling and want to help solve whatever it is that they are struggling with, but sometimes the best thing you can do is sit on the sidelines and let them figure it out, no matter how painful is for you or your child.

Your sixteen-year-old gets their first job, and they are often late for their shift or don't fulfill their responsibilities. You offer advice in the beginning, but their behaviors continue. As their parent, you can see this will end badly for your child, but it's not your job to fix it. In fact, just the opposite. You job is to let them experience the natural consequences of their irresponsibility. Two weeks into their new job, they call you, crying that they have just been fired. You feel terrible for them, but it doesn't change the fact that this consequence is a result of their poor choices. The best thing you can do is empathize with them. "I feel bad for you. That's unfortunate." And then you can help them reflect on their choices and how they could do better in the future. "How could you be a better employee at your next job?"

Your nine-year-old has a friend over to play. You observe that your child gets mad whenever they lose a game or will only play games that they want to play. Their friend is getting frustrated and decides to go home early. Your child is upset that their friend left. Offer empathy: "It's hard when someone doesn't want to play with us." And then help them reflect on their choices and how they could do better in the future. "Why do you think they wanted to leave early? How could you be a better friend the next time you play together?"

No matter the age of your child, parenting is a tough job, and a constant one. That you have read this book means you want to be a better parent for your children. That's a tremendous first step; acknowledge it, and then start making plans for what's next!

Reflections

- *Review your list of emotions and the situations that prompted them. Are you experiencing these emotions more frequently than you realized? How does that make you feel?*

- *Dig deeper into one of your emotional reactions:*

  - *Why do you think that situation triggered your emotion?*

▫ *Close your eyes and imagine that situation. As your anger, anxiety, or fear begins to bubble up, practice one of the breathing exercises.*

▫ *Now imagine that situation and taking the steps to "reset" your vagus nerve the moment your emotions begin to bubble up. How would that reset allow you to address that situation in a calm and rational way that is best for your child?*

· *Continue to note when you are experience emotions that do not fit the situation and practice resetting your vagus nerve through calming exercises that work for you. You may need to try a variety of exercises before you find the ones that are most effective for you.*

Conclusion

N ot long ago, a mom called into our office to schedule an appointment for her son. When our practice manager asked for her son's name, age, and date of birth, she said, "Jason. He's thirty-one."

Our practice manager stopped her before she could go any further. "I'm sorry, but your son will need to call us to set up his own appointment."

"But I make all his appointments," she said.

Once the mother understood we would only book the appointment with her son, she hung up, and Jason called back ten minutes later. Jason stumbled through the call, pausing a few times to ask his mother about his insurance information. "My mom usually does this stuff," he said by way of explanation. I've since met Jason, and I want to be clear that this was not an adult who had limitations that prevented him from communicating for himself—he had no clue how because his mother had always done it for him.

By now, I hope we can all agree that this should not be the endgame every parent should be working toward, yet it often is and will continue to be if we don't break this widespread pattern of hypervigilant parenting. We can, should, and must do better for our children. You're still reading, so I know you want to. My hope is that this book has you not just thinking differently about how you parent but has inspired the confidence to take action.

I encourage you to review the "Take a Moment" and "Reflection" exercises you did throughout the book and begin to map out your next steps. For some, that may be sharing this book with their partner. For others, it may be taking a parenting class or researching counseling options. Whatever your next steps are, remember there are supports out there to help you through the process—please don't go it alone.

In the hard moments and in the moments you don't get it "right," be kind to yourself, give yourself grace, and take the opportunity learn from those moments. Remember to breathe.

Take the Parenting Style Assessment

Ready to gain insights into yourself and your parenting style?

Take the parenting style assessment by following the QR code below.

Acknowledgements

♥

There are so many people I need to acknowledge that helped me get to where I am today. The first person that jumps to my mind is my daughter, Amethyst. She was the reason I realized I had to change how I parented and needed to deal with my childhood trauma and get healthy. She pushes me each day to become a better person and a better mother. Without her, this book would not exist.

Next would be my wonderful partner in life, Steve. He has always believed in me and been willing to support my decisions. More importantly, he was willing to learn and grow with me to become a better parent. With him I was able to be so much more, and I would be lost without his love and daily support.

To my sweet granddaughter, Madison, she is the light of my life and reminds me that even with all my skill and knowledge, parenting is hard. As I wrote this book, I would often be humbled by her and her clever ways. She helped remind me to make sure that anyone reading this book would get the message: parenting is hard.

To all the foster children who have been a part of my life — I am not allowed to share names due to confidentiality — they all molded a part of this book. From them I learned about attachment, bonding, and support. They also taught me patience and tolerance are very important when working with all children, but especially with children who have difficult lives.

Thank you to my parents and siblings for being a part of my life. If I had not had these experiences, I would not be who I am today. Some of the lessons I learned growing up with my family are shared in this book.

My dear friends, Cyndi, Thomas, and Lisa who have always believed in me, no matter what hair-brained scheme I plan on doing next. Each of them has been a sounding board, a shoulder to cry on, or someone to laugh with, and I am blessed to have them. They gave me the confidence to keep going with this book even when I believed it was a huge mistake.

To Mr. Cuellar, a teacher that was so instrumental in me feeling cared about when I was young. I am positive he will never know the impact he had on me, but I was a very shy and scared little girl. He demonstrated that he cared about me each day and helped cultivate my love of books by reading to us and encouraging me to read. It is this reading habit that helped me begin to find ways to heal, led me to my career as a mental health therapist, and motivated me to write this book.

Thank you, Advantage Media Group, who without them this book would still be sitting in my Google Drive with the heading, "someday." They helped me see it was possible to write a book and provided the tools to make it happen

Finally, to Beth, without your help, guidance, incredible skill, support, encouragement, and talent this book would not have been anywhere near as great as it is, thank you. You are a true wordsmith.

Printed in the USA
CPSIA information can be obtained
at www.ICGtesting.com
JSHW021443030823
45895JS00002B/16